Books by Vivian Grey

THE FIRST BOOK OF ASTRONOMY

SECRET OF THE MYSTERIOUS RAYS:
THE DISCOVERY OF NUCLEAR ENERGY

THE INVISIBLE GIANTS: ATOMS, NUCLEI, AND RADIOISOTOPES

ROENTGEN'S REVOLUTION: THE DISCOVERY OF THE X RAY

ROENTGEN'S REVOLUTION

The Discovery of the X Ray

Wilhelm Conrad Roentgen

ROENTGEN'S REVOLUTION

The Discovery of the X Ray

VIVIAN GREY

Little, Brown and Company · Boston · Toronto

FIRST EDITION
T 06/73

*Wilhelm Conrad Roentgen and the Early History of the Roentgen
Rays* by Otto Glasser, Copyright © 1934, was used as the source
for original passages from letters, articles and statements by
Roentgen and his contemporaries. Courtesy of Charles C. Thomas,
Publisher, Springfield, Illinois.

Library of Congress Cataloging in Publication Data

Grey, Vivian.
    Roentgen's revolution.

    SUMMARY: The biography of the German physicist
who accidentally discovered the x ray and won the
Nobel Prize for physics in 1901.
    1. Röntgen, Wilhelm Conrad, 1845–1923—Juvenile
literature. 2. X-rays—Juvenile literature.
[1. Röntgen, Wilhelm Conrad, 1845–1923. 2. Physicists.
3. X rays] I. Title.
QC16.R47G7   530'.092'4 [B] [92]   73-3153
ISBN 0-316-32821-9

*Published simultaneously in Canada
by Little, Brown & Company (Canada) Limited*

PRINTED IN THE UNITED STATES OF AMERICA

To my daughters Jackie and Leslie
— and to what this is all about

Acknowledgments

With the request that his papers be burned, Wilhelm Conrad Roentgen destroyed forever many materials that could have helped us better understand him.

Fortunately, though, Dr. Otto Glasser, Professor of Biophysics at the Cleveland Clinic Foundation until his death in 1964, gathered letters Roentgen had written to others, who had saved them. He also collected newspaper and magazine articles written about the rays at the time of their discovery. Combining all of this with some comments from Roentgen's friends and associates, Dr. Glasser authored *Wilhelm Conrad Roentgen and the Early History of the Roentgen Rays*, which was published first in Germany in 1931, later in England in 1933, and in America in 1934.

I obtained much of this material, particularly Roentgen's quotes, from Dr. Glasser's book. I also consulted the *Encyclopedia of X Rays and Gamma Rays*, edited by G. Clark, the article "Wilhelm Conrad Roentgen: On a New Kind of Rays" by Herbert S. Klickstein, which appeared in Volume I of *Mallinckrodt Classics of Radiology* (1960), and a book by Bern Dibner, *Wilhelm Conrad Roentgen and the Discovery of the X Ray* (New York: Franklin Watts, 1968). My search led me to Utrecht and Apeldoorn,

ACKNOWLEDGMENTS

Holland, to correspondences with the "Keeper of the Public Records" of both cities, and to many members of the scientific community. To all who shared their information, insights and memories with me, I wish to now formally extend my gratitude and thanks.

And most of all, I am deeply grateful to my daughters, Leslie and Jackie, for never once doubting that I could piece together a book that began with a few singular scraps of information and a curiosity about the man who forced a revolution in physics and ultimately changed the course of the world.

V. G.

Contents

1. Troubles with Teachers 3
2. Growing Up 7
3. Troubles with Schools 13
4. False Starts 18
5. Fresh Hopes 22
6. College Life 26
7. What Next? 33
8. Troubles with Parents 39
9. Beginning It All 44
10. The Experimenter 47
11. Würzburg Changes Its Mind 59
12. The Good Life 65
13. X Rays 72
14. The Search 80
15. Unnoticed 85
16. Center of the Storm 88
17. Convincing the World 93
18. Price of Fame 99
19. Problems, Rumors, and Rewards 107
20. The Nobel Prize 112
21. Bertha 118
22. The Lonely Years 128
23. Epilogue: And Afterwards 133

Important Dates in the Life of Wilhelm Conrad Roentgen

His Excellency, Geheimrat Professor Dr. Wilhelm Conrad Roentgen:

1845   Born on March 27, at Lennep.

1868   Diploma of mechanical engineer, Zurich.

1869   Ph.D., Zurich, June.

1872   Married Bertha Ludwig, January.

1872   *Privatdozent* at the University of Strasbourg, March 13.

1875   Professor at the Agricultural School at Hohenheim, April 1.

1876   Associate professor at the University of Strasbourg, October 1.

1879   Professor of Physics at the University of Giessen, April 1.

1888   Professor of Physics at the University of Würzburg, October 1.

1894   Rector at the University of Würzburg.

1895   X rays.

1900   Professor of Physics at the University of Munich, April 1. Director of the Physical Institute of the University of Munich, conservator of the Physical-Metronomical Institute of the State of Bavaria, member of the Board of Governors of the Physikalisch-Technische Reichsanstalt in Charlottenburg.

Ritter of the Verdienst Orden (Royal Merit) of the Bavarian Crown, the Grosskomturkreuz of the Verdienst Orden, recipient of the Verdienst Orden of Saint Michael I, of the Silver Medal of Prinz Regent Luitpold, of the Ordre pour le Mérite for Science and Art, of the Prussian Kronenorden II, Komtur of the Order of the Italian Crown, and member of the Maximilian Order for Science with Decoration.

1901 Nobel Prize for physics.

1923 Died on February 10, at Munich.

1

Troubles with Teachers

Have you ever started off to school in the morning not expecting anything unusual to happen, and by the end of the day wondered how you possibly could have gotten into so much trouble?

It was that way for sixteen-year-old Wilhelm Conrad Roentgen. One day he would be among the world's most respected scientists, best known for his discovery of the X ray.

But when the disaster began, no one, especially his schoolmaster, suspected that Wilhelm would become famous. There certainly was no hint of Wilhelm's future scientific greatness when his troubles started.

He was studying at the gymnasium, a private school in Utrecht, the Netherlands. The gymnasium was a classical school, the only school to attend if you wanted to go on to a university. Most of the students entered there at twelve years of age and their course of study lasted six years, until they were eighteen years old.

Wilhelm, like all the boys in his class, was at the gym-

3

nasium for only two reasons: to pass the grim and difficult entrance examination of the University of Utrecht and to get a *Matura*, the high-school diploma. It was the law, in 1861, that every student applying to a university had to satisfy two requirements: he had to pass its competitive entrance examination, and he had to present the *Matura*. Only if he had a *Matura* could a student prove that he had graduated from a state-approved school and had passed all the state-required courses.

For as long as he could remember, Wilhelm had been going to school so that one day he could enter the university. When the trouble began he knew he had to endure only two more years at the preparatory school.

As he started out that morning, Wilhelm had no way of knowing it would not be just another ordinary dreary day at school. But no matter how important or how famous he was to become, he would never forget that eventful day nor the days that followed.

As he came into the classroom on that special day, his classmates were crowding around the fire screen in front of the stove. Joining them, he could understand why. The fire screen was being newly "decorated." One of the other students was drawing a figure of their schoolmaster on it.

The decoration was a chalk drawing — really a caricature — of their teacher. It was not a real likeness of the form master, but a picture which exaggerated his peculiarities and defects.

Wilhelm was all the more fascinated by the sketch because he was not an artist. In fact, he knew everyone always considered him rather poor in drawing.

4

Just as his friend was about to finish, the teacher suddenly appeared.

The furious form master began to question the class. Which student had made the sketch?

All at once, what began as a harmless joke suddenly turned into something quite different.

All of them silently stared at the teacher.

He repeated the question.

Still the silence.

The teacher would not give up.

Like so many of the older men Wilhelm knew in Utrecht, the form master had no sense of humor. Although Wilhelm's family enjoyed a good joke, most of the other adults he knew did not appreciate or even understand one.

The schoolmaster saw nothing clever in the sketch or in the humor of the drawing. To him the situation was growing to much more than just a prank. Now, he insisted, the class was disobeying his orders.

With each second of silence, the mood grew more and more tense. Neither side seemed ready to give in.

Sitting among his soundless classmates Wilhelm weighed the possibilities of punishment. What could and would the form master do? He knew the teacher could not beat him, corporal punishment was no longer allowed by law, and besides, most parents were really against it. These days students received detention or were given some unpleasant job to do after school.

The hushed class made no sound. Still their teacher stormed around the room.

The culprit remained just as quiet as the rest.

Never really knowing why, or what put the idea into his head, but only knowing that he wanted to put a stop to the senseless situation, Wilhelm spoke up.

He admitted the crime.

Wilhelm knew deep down his teacher could not possibly believe his confession. Everyone knew he was not skilled or talented enough to draw that clever caricature.

His "confession" was over. Now the punishment.

But the sentence didn't come right away. His crime had been too severe. This time the punishment would not come from his teacher but from the director of the entire gymnasium. As soon as it could be arranged, the director would hear his crime and decide on a fitting sentence. In the meantime, he was suspended from school.

And so what began as an ordinary uneventful school day at nine A.M. had changed into a nightmare for Wilhelm Conrad Roentgen. By the end of the day he found himself in complete disgrace and suspended from school.

Wilhelm was caught between two worlds. Whose side should he take? Who was more wrong? The form master who knew he could not have drawn the caricature on the fire screen and yet insisted on punishing him because he needed a culprit? Or his good friend, the "artistic" classmate who would not own up to the crime and was content to let him take the blame?

2

Growing Up

How do you tell your parents you are suspended from school? That you might even be expelled?

This was not the first time Wilhelm had to tell his parents that he was in trouble at school. But it promised to be the worst mess he had ever been in. He had been involved in disturbances before. Sometimes he was even known as a problem boy.

But this time it was all different. It was much more serious. This time the director himself was to pass sentence. What made it all the more unreasonable was that for this one time he was really innocent. He had not really caused any trouble. And he was sure the schoolmaster knew it.

He tried to imagine: what would the punishment be? In spite of what appeared to be strict supervision by the teachers, he and the other students knew deep down that there was not much discipline in the school. This was never really said out loud. It was just understood. Wilhelm knew he could play endless jokes just as long as he did nothing to make the teachers want to expel him from school. Considering it carefully, he could not see that a chalk drawing of a teacher was a prank harmful enough to cause them to expel him.

But nothing this serious had ever happened to him before. He was always able to get out of trouble. For that matter, ever since he could remember, he always had had an easy time of it. Even when his friends were sick with chicken pox and measles, all those childhood diseases, he was always the healthy one who managed to escape them.

He was sure that the threat of being expelled was just a warning meant to worry him, and little more. Of course he would be allowed to graduate.

Most of his life was already all planned out for him by his family. Ever since he could remember, it seemed, his future had been decided by them. Of course he never questioned their decision. Why should he? Nor did it occur to him to want to change their plans. Without any-one ever really insisting, he knew exactly what was in store for the next few years. He was just one more boy coming from the wealthy upper-class family of burghers, expecting one day to come into the family business or to enter a good profession.

Wilhelm knew he had come from a long line of people who were successful and respected in business. All his relatives were used to a good way of life, used to fine food, fine homes and a bit of fun. Although all were

8

known to be hardworking, he knew they also enjoyed a good joke. The family was easygoing, not demanding, yet expecting and getting the best out of life. His grandfather had once been mayor of the Prussian city of Lennep. His father, Freidrich Conrad Roentgen, had also been born in Lennep. For that matter, he too had been born in Lennep, on March 27, 1845, at 4 P.M., in his parents' attractive frame house at No. 287 Postrasse.

But in spite of all those strong ties to Lennep, Wilhelm could barely remember the city. When he was three years old, in 1848, his parents sold their house to Gustav Kunmen. Hoping to find better business conditions, his father moved the three of them to the Netherlands. When he did, his father gave up the family's Prussian citizenship and they all became citizens of the Netherlands.

The weather in Holland was sometimes chilly, even downright raw in May and June. But mid-spring was the time of glory in the tulip fields. Bundled in warm clothes, Wilhelm was later told, he and his parents had arrived in Apeldoorn, the central Netherlands, when the last of the tulips were flowering.

Apeldoorn, where he lived before coming to Utrecht, gave the impression of being largely a garden or park with a city hidden somewhere among the leaves, trees, and flowers. There were about nine thousand people living there in 1848. Many of the men were farmers, cattle breeders, or sheep raisers. There were also about forty paper mills and some other little industries.

Just as his father's family was known and respected in

9

Lennep, his mother's family was equally well known in Apeldoorn. They, too, had first lived in Prussia and then moved to the Netherlands.

Wilhelm could remember that cottage in Apeldoorn, in the Hoofstraat. Their house was filled with paintings, most of them old Dutch; in fact, one painting of the Holy Family was even considered to be an art treasure. His mother loved to display their beautiful old pieces of silver hollowware, Wedgwood and Meissen china, a collection of old Chinese pictures which one of her ancestors had brought back from a trip to the Orient, old Chinese china, mahogany furniture and a few chairs from the eighteenth century.

In those years when he was growing up and going to school there, Apeldoorn had one public elementary school, one charity school, two day and boarding schools and one day school for girls.

Wilhelm was only dimly aware that there were other boys his age who lived a very different kind of life from his. They were the boys whose families lived on houseboats on the canals. These boys would live out their lives on barges on water, perhaps never going to land except to pull the barges full of cheese, vegetables and flowers up and down the canals.

Compared to them, he knew he had an easy time of it. After his preliminary schooling, his parents sent him to the best school in Apeldoorn, the Institute of Martinus Herman van Doorn.

No one had to wear a school uniform there. All of them

studied the French and Dutch languages, figures, geography, general and Dutch history. At this school there was no Greek or Latin education, which was compulsory for the university. Although Wilhelm's family couldn't know it, this lack of Greek or Latin would prove to be a mark against Wilhelm for the rest of his life.

Wilhelm and his classmates learned early that the institute was known as a school mainly reserved for the wealthy. For the day school, the tuition came to forty Dutch florins, or ninety-five dollars, a year for one child, and for the boarding school, to two hundred and seventy-five Dutch florins, or six hundred and thirty dollars, a year for one child.

The high cost of sending Wilhelm to the institute was worth it to his parents, for the school board of Apeldoorn was exceedingly content with the lessons of Mr. van Doorn. In the government return of 1856, this board wrote that he had "the gift to fill his pupils with desire and diligence for their work."

There were almost never more than six boys to a class and often the pupils were taught one by one. Wilhelm could remember that each day's work was differently arranged for each boy. Some of the lessons lasted for an hour, the rest were three-quarters of an hour long. They all went to school about nine and a half hours a day. The only grades were the ones from the last examination. And Wilhelm's grades were not too good. He knew he was not considered a rapid student at the institute.

Later, he would be told he was best remembered for

his great love for nature and for roaming through Apeldoorn's forests and fields with his friends. On second thought, though, some did remember he did have a special gift for making all sorts of mechanical gadgets.

He designed an especially good gadget for smoking. All the schoolboys enjoyed smoking cigars and did so as early as they could. In fact, it was not unusual to see them smoking cigars as they played their after-school sports. When Wilhelm was first permitted to smoke, he received a beautiful meerschaum holder from his uncle and constructed a little suction pump with which he quickly and automatically seasoned it.

After completing his studies at the institute, Wilhelm knew exactly what the next step would be in his education: he would go on to attend a more advanced school, called a gymnasium. And, exactly as expected, he did leave Apeldoorn and move to Utrecht to continue the next step in his schooling.

For years now, he had been living with friends of his parents and going to the gymnasium. Nothing in his life, so far, had been unpleasant, unexpected, or unplanned.

Even though he was now suspended from school until the director would see him, Wilhelm was not too worried. He did not believe anything unusual or disastrous would ever happen to him.

And so, secure and not at all frightened, confident and not at all upset, Wilhelm arrived at the gymnasium to come before the director and to receive his punishment.

3

Troubles with Schools

On a day that would scar his memory forever, Wilhelm entered the office of the director of the gymnasium. Behind the closed door the form master presented his case. The director and the teachers came to a verdict. As the director passed judgment Wilhelm listened, hoping he wasn't really hearing what was said.

Wilhelm was expelled — not for a day or for a week or even for a month. He was expelled for all time, forever. He would never be permitted to return to the gymnasium.

All knew what this edict meant. Expulsion meant he could never take the state examinations, could never graduate or earn a diploma. Without finishing these requirements, he could not enter a university.

Because of the cartoon on the fire screen, the whole course of his life would have to change. All his plans and dreams, it seemed, were over.

His name would never appear in the *Album Discipulorium* of the Stedelijl Gymnasium in Utrecht, nor on the list of pupils of any of the gymnasia in the entire province of Gelderland.

How many times then and in the years to come would he ask himself: why did I confess? And, once he had admitted he was guilty, should he have told the real truth? Did he make the right choice?

For the rest of his life Wilhelm would bristle over the form master who had taken a harmless prank — especially one done by someone else — and magnified it until he was expelled and his life changed forever.

It did not take long for the news to travel back to his parents in Apeldoorn. There was nothing to do but tell them that their only son had been expelled from school in complete disgrace.

But whatever his mother and father may have said to each other in private, Wilhelm knew they defended him to the world. His mother, especially, was one of the few who stood by him. She insisted she had complete confidence in him.

For the first time there was a sense of hopelessness about everything for him. The laws of his country were clear and strict. Obey them and there would be no trouble. But just try to do something different, or to change a law, and you would feel its power. Nothing, it seemed, or no one, could change the school system for him alone. The director's sentence was final.

Now that its doors were forever closed to him, he wanted to go to the university more than anything he had ever wanted to do. He could not remember ever wanting something and not having it. Now, suddenly,

14

the very thing he wanted most, the one thing most important to him for the rest of his life, was to be denied.

Neither he, nor his parents, nor his parents' influential friends, could change the school's verdict. The director, representing the government, had made a decision about his future. Whether he wanted to or not, Wilhelm would have to obey it.

This is what made the verdict all the more difficult to swallow. He did not believe the decision was a fair one. He could not understand how a learned director could deliver such an unfair verdict. At school he had always been taught to be truthful and fair-minded. Yet it seemed that his teachers were now going against their own teachings.

Much as the three of them hated to, he and his parents had to begin to consider what he should do next. He knew he didn't want to go back home to Apeldoorn. He was not ready to settle down and go to work. For the first time in his life, he wanted only one thing — to go back to school.

But then a friend told his parents that an exception might be made so that Wilhelm could take a private entrance examination to the university. If he was successful and passed it, he would be permitted to enter the university even without the *Matura*.

Clinging to this one last hope, they decided that Wilhelm should try the one chance left open to him. He should study at home and then attempt to pass that examination.

The date for the private examination was arranged. They hired a teacher for him.

The weeks before the exam he and his instructor studied every possible subject.

He never had tried to learn so much, to cram so many facts into his head before. He was prepared with answers in a way he never would have been otherwise.

As the day for the test came closer, he was reminded over and over again, then warned over and over again, that this would be his absolute last chance.

He was told the name of his examiner. It was to be one of the teachers from his gymnasium who was favorable to him. Certainly this was a good omen.

Many of the answers were to be spoken rather than written. It would be up to the questioner to decide, after listening to him, whether Wilhelm knew what he was talking about. If the examiner was someone who liked Wilhelm it would be all to the good.

Even so, he knew nothing must be left to chance.

He had to remember everything.

He knew he had to do more than his best.

The rest of his life rested on the exam he would take, the answers he would give.

At last, he looked at the last book for the last time.

The exam was scheduled for the next day.

Then he heard the news. The teacher who was to give him the exam was sick. The substitute examiner was one of the very teachers who helped expel him from the gymnasium.

wrote ourselves. On holidays we always had happy, gay entertainment. That was a pleasant and profitable time! . . . Coming back once more to those years of my youth, I should like to add that I went horseback riding, skating, and indulged in other forms of physical exercise. . . .

Although he didn't want them to know it, and he was shy about saying anything, he admired their daughter a great deal. Even so, he'd play tricks on her whenever he could. He would take her shoes from the door and hide them. Or, when her boyfriend would come, he would parade in front of both wearing the most ragged old clothes he could find.

The house he was living in was clean and neat, but then Wilhelm took the neatness of the Dutch houses for granted. He hardly noticed the housewives of Holland, who were famous for scrubbing every inch of their homes every day.

Until now, he had been going from day to day hardly aware of the sameness of everything. He had traveled to and from the gymnasium for the past four years, passing the straight trees fringing the roads through the canals and their smells, passing the dikes, dams, sluices and windmills, and passing the seemingly indestructible rooted houses.

Nearly one-half of his country was below sea level. Water was the ever-present, ever-threatening problem — too much water wherever he looked.

Almost everything except the old parish churches, the town hall, the trees and the dikes were all little and small-scaled. The flatness of a land surrounded by water waiting to suck up the soil was something he learned to take for granted.

Even the weather followed the same pattern. In the summer it was the mist which enveloped meadow and street alike after a warm day, or in the winter it was the same sunlessness day after day.

But in spite of the sameness, Wilhelm learned that if you really looked and listened there were differences. The way a man spoke would tell you what section of the country he came from and whether or not he had ever received an education. What he wore told you even more than his speech, and where he lived told you the most about him.

Since everything in the Netherlands was so much the same, he might as well remain in Utrecht. Even though the law said he could not attend the university, it did not say that he could not attend other schools. If he wished, he could enter a technical school.

Wilhelm and his family knew that if he went to a technical school, he was accepting a lot more than a change of schools or a shift in education. It meant that for the rest of his life he would be doing a lower type of work than he had hoped for. It also meant he was accepting a lower social class and station in life.

The system finally had its own way. Now it was forcing him to accept second best in life.

But there was nothing else he could do.

He took the examination for the technical institute.

Like nearly every examination, it was a government affair. This time he passed it.

On December 5, 1862, Wilhelm moved away from his parents' friends. He went to live with Dr. J. W. Gunning, a well-known professor of chemistry. Since 1855 Dr. Gunning had been a chemistry teacher at the technical school of Utrecht.

Three weeks later, on December 27, Wilhelm entered the technical school.

This was a higher type of technical school. It prepared its fifty-five male students for entrance into the Technological University of Delft or for an agricultural college or a school of economics. The boys were taught fourteen subjects spread over a week of thirty-six lessons. There was either a two- or three-year course. All learned some mathematics, natural science, modern languages and commercial subjects. Wilhelm, at eighteen, was one of the older students.

With this trade school, all hopes for Wilhelm for becoming a scholar or a scientist were gone. And by now he was beginning to realize that was what he really wanted to do for the rest of his life.

5

Fresh Hopes

The three years at the technical school flew by. When Wilhelm graduated, he didn't celebrate with the rest of his class. The others were content with their lot in life. But he still wanted more.

On January 18, 1865, he entered the University of Utrecht at last. But not as a regular student. He could attend all classes, but he would never get a degree. The list of students of the Rhine Territory, called the *Album studiosorum Rheno-Traiectina*, Utrecht, 1866, mentions him as entering as a student of philosophy from *pravata instutione uses est*, or a private institution.

The whole university system was destined to prepare the student for his final examination and that was all. Classes were open to all who paid the necessary fees, which were small. But the degree Wilhelm wanted, the degree of doctor, could only be granted to those who had earlier passed the gymnasium final or the equivalent examination. And he had failed to do either.

FRESH HOPES

As he told a friend when he was older:

In order not to lose touch with science, I registered myself
as an auditor at Utrecht University. There I attended lectures
on physics, chemistry and zoology. In the summer of 1865,
I began to consider seriously which town would be the most
suitable for my later training as a machine engineer, since
this career seemed to fit in best with my interests and learning. Obviously it was not Utrecht.

Utrecht University was like all the other universities in
Holland. It had opened in 1636 and although it was over
two hundred years old, there were no beautiful buildings,
no rival colleges, no tutors or proctors, and no university
gate.

The university was managed entirely by the state,
which paid the professors and provided the necessary
buildings. The subjects to be taught and the examinations
to be held in the various colleges were laid down by law.

This meant that the professors, though very learned
men, did not enjoy any great social standing, and their
title did not carry with it anything like the same rank it
would in other countries.

Most of the faculty did not mix easily or at all with the
students. The professors gave their lectures and saw little
of their students outside the classroom.

Wilhelm quickly joined the famous student circle,
Naturadux nobis et auspax, which means "Nature is our
leader and our guide." Most of the circles were really
fencing clubs whose members fought duels with each
other. Almost all the students joined a circle.

Sometimes Wilhelm caught himself thinking as if he were a regular student at the university. But all too often he remembered how unreal his dream actually was.

And then, out of nowhere, someone he met quite casually and might never see again, just as casually told him about a way that he could get that dreamed-of university diploma.

A Swiss engineer named Thormann, whom Wilhelm happened to meet and tell his troubles to, advised him to try to apply to the Polytechnic Institute in Zurich, Switzerland.

The Polytechnic Institute, Thormann told him, did not require the usual certificate, the all-important *Matura*. If the applicant could pass their unusually difficult entrance examination, the Polytechnic Institute did not insist on the graduation papers. Wilhelm would not need a *Matura* here before he could apply.

As he put it years later:

Quite by chance, I made the acquaintance of a Swiss engineer named Thormann. I told him of my dilemma and he explained to me that at the Federal Polytechnic Institute in Zurich it was possible for pupils with aptitude to study, even without the *Matura*. This proved my saving grace, and was something which exceeded my wildest dreams.

In double-quick time he applied to the Polytechnic Institute. Now at last he would have a chance to earn a degree as a scientist.

For the first time he would be admitted as a regular student to a school he wanted to attend.

didn't go to class each time, it didn't matter; he had only to appear for and take exams.

Sometimes the two took hiking trips in the mountains through deep, newly fallen snow. Then, Wilhelm led the way, loving the idea that he never knew what kind of dangers lay hidden, buried underfoot. Sometimes when he pressed forward, he could hear his exasperated friend falling farther and farther behind, scolding and shouting that Wilhelm's legs were too long and his strides were too huge.

Although the mountains always overshadowed them, Wilhelm knew that if he went far enough beyond the busy city of Zurich, those cloud-reaching peaks would shrink into gentle slopes of shocked wheat and ripening vegetables.

Even though it was also a small country like Holland, the Swiss were different from the people in Holland, and he liked them.

Back home in Holland, all the streets, all the canals, all the people, were always the same. But Switzerland, which was just as small, was a country of opposites. The Swiss were a people who were not interested in becoming like one another. Instead of wanting everyone to be the same, it seemed that the Swiss were eager to show their differences. It was as if they had discovered that it was just more practical to let the other man go his own way.

And that suited Wilhelm just fine.

It was just as well for him that the Swiss did believe in minding their own business. For the first time in years

Wilhelm was back to his old self again. He was playing jokes again, and loving the good life again, just as he had once done in Utrecht. And he liked to have his own way, especially when spending money. Even though both the Dutch and Swiss believed you should save money, Wilhelm spent it when, where and how he pleased.

For instance, one summer he and his Dutch friend ordered white suits and hats made for themselves. This was an unheard of extravagance. On Sundays the pair strolled about in their white finery. Both enjoyed the walks even more knowing they were shocking the thrifty Zurich townsfolk.

Another time they both thought they were in love with the same actress. Neither of them knew her, but both bought huge bouquets of red roses and took them to her apartment. She opened the door, but they both were so embarrassed they couldn't talk. Shoving the flowers at her, they disappeared.

Of the pair, though, Wilhelm knew his friend was the better talker. Later, his friend managed to meet the actress, and even dated her.

Besides buying expensive white suits, flowers, or anything else he wanted, Wilhelm used to love to hire horses and would drive a four-horse carriage through the streets of Zurich as often as possible. Of course it was expensive. He didn't care.

But in spite of all the fun, large parties didn't interest him. He preferred meeting and talking to a few of his friends. He didn't like to dance, either.

Somewhere along the way, he picked up the nickname

"Apeldoorn," after his hometown in Holland. Soon most of his friends, even several of the younger, unmarried professors called him "Apeldoorn."

After classes he and the other students and some professors usually met to have a cool drink or to down large quantities of that strong Swiss coffee. One of their favorite cafés was the Zum Grunen Glas. Its owner, Johann Gottfried Ludwig, often tutored students in languages and in fencing, and sometimes even translated their theses into Latin for them.

Almost before he realized it, by the end of 1866, Wilhelm was returning to that café more and more often. But it wasn't for the cool drinks or a talk with its proprietor. It was because of Herr G. Ludwig's middle daughter.

Anna Bertha Ludwig was six years older than he. But he didn't care; he was most interested in her. Bertha was tall and slender, with a twinkle in her eyes, and she always wore a smile. Her willingness to laugh, to enjoy life, were so like his — and so different from the dour Swiss or the calm Dutch.

It didn't take him long to decide: someday he would marry Bertha.

Even thinking about getting married meant that he was beginning to think more seriously about life. It was coming over him so slowly that he didn't really know it was happening. All at once, though, he noticed that he was doing more and more work at school. In some cases, he was even doing more than was expected of him.

Most of his classes were on mathematics and chemistry

and were difficult enough. Yet he began going to lectures on still another science — physics. The science of physics was the basic science from which all other sciences developed. It was concerned with the world of things and actions.

Those lectures on physics were given by Professor Rudolf Clausius. The professor was one of the first experimenters in thermodynamics, a new branch of physics. The researchers knew, now, that heat and work were both different forms of energy. Thermodynamics was the study of the relationship between heat and work and how to change one form of energy into the other. Professor Clausius was a pioneer in developing the new heat engines which were being built because of what was being learned about thermodynamics. Certainly it was all very complicated, but Wilhelm found that he was especially impressed with the clearness of Professor Clausius's lectures and by the experiments he demonstrated to the class.

But no matter how many classes he went to, Wilhelm was forced to face the fact that he could never make up what he missed by being expelled from the gymnasium. This was especially true of languages; he realized he did not have and would never have a systematic education in the classical languages. Yet, mastery of Latin and Greek was the sign of a truly educated man, according to most university traditions.

What else was there to do but to memorize some Latin and Greek passages? As the years passed, he began to use the few Latin phrases he learned, impressing others as if he really did know the language.

Wilhelm's earlier school years weren't all wasted — not even the work at the Utrecht technical school, where he learned the practical parts of machines. Times around 1866 were changing and machines were becoming more and more important. Some people were calling these times the Industrial Revolution. Already the need for more yarn and cloth had led to the introduction of textile machinery; the need for more coal to the first steam engines; the need for cheap transportation to the improvement of ports, canals, roads, bridges and to the radical new railroads. The steam engine, first developed for pumping, was adapted now to other uses, such as blowing furnaces and hammering iron and was replacing the water wheel in driving machinery.

Wilhelm liked doing what was new and exciting. He wanted to change with the times, and that meant becoming an engineer; more than that, a mechanical engineer — a man who worked with machines. As a mechanical engineer, Wilhelm would work in some way on the smooth performance of machines — putting into practice many of the ideas he heard in Professor Clausius's lectures. As a mechanical engineer, he hoped to be part of the new and exciting world of machines.

Before he knew it, two, then three years passed, and it was 1868. Wilhelm knew that soon he would graduate and would have a certificate saying he was a graduate mechanical engineer.

But he was beginning to face it: he had to admit it to himself. He really didn't want to be a mechanical engineer after all. He had changed his mind.

What he was considering would mean going on with even more schooling. Should he, in spite of his patchwork education, try to become a true scientist? Should he go on and try for the highest degree, the most difficult degree of all to earn, the Ph.D?

With these questions unanswered, many decisions put off, and his future plans still fuzzy, Wilhelm graduated from the Zurich Polytechnic Institute.

He had a diploma in his pocket. Even if it was only his mechanical engineer's diploma, it was at least something secure, whatever the future might bring. At last the bitter battle he and his parents had fought together was over. He had graduated at last.

Somehow, though, the triumph of graduation was not all that he expected. It was almost as if he were some kind of athlete — working and training for a sports event and finally winning it. Built right into the triumph of winning and of graduation was the question, "What do I do now?"

7

What Next?

Now he must face it. He must make up his mind. Should he go to work as a mechanical engineer, or should he go on with even more schooling?

A few years earlier, in Utrecht, the choice would have been an easy one. But now in Zurich, at the Polytechnic Institute, he had met professors who, for the first time, had made going to school interesting and worthwhile to him.

It was really the study of physics, the science dealing with natural laws and processes, which kept pulling him back to more studies and more school. It certainly wasn't the idea that someday he might make a great new scientific discovery in physics that kept his interest; Wilhelm knew all physicists believed that almost everything in science could be explained by the rules and theories they already knew. If something did not seem to fit in with what the scientists knew to be true, or something odd happened in an experiment, there was nothing to worry about. No doubt it would turn out to be explainable if only someone with enough imagination would try to explain it. To Wilhelm, to everyone in 1868, the study of physics would soon be complete except for the addition of more decimal points to measurements.

And just then he met another who would have a marked influence on him. He would tell about that important meeting years later:

> At this critical time I became acquainted with a young professor of physics, Kundt, who asked me one day, "What really are your plans for the future?" When I answered that I didn't know he told me to try physical science; when I admitted that I had spent very little time in physics, he replied that this probably could be remedied. In short, at the age of twenty-four years, and already practically engaged, I began to experiment and to study physics.

Wilhelm had to weigh his decision carefully. Not only did he have to decide whether or not to continue with school, but where should he go? He knew he could not remain at the Polytechnic Institute any longer. In order to earn a Ph.D., he would have to apply to the University of Zurich. And he knew only too well that he would be refused. He had been all through it too many times before. He did not have a *Matura*, and he had not received the classical education which the university required.

Although he could not qualify as a student at the university, he carefully read their rules and discovered that it did not say he could not write a thesis and try for the Ph.D. anyway.

Someday he would recall:

WHAT NEXT?

My old love for experimental physics was born anew. The next step would have been to have continued my studies in physics, begun at the Polytechnic. But I wanted to have another try at a university. I had long known that matriculation was out of the question; at the same time, it was possible for me, according to the rules, to obtain my degree if I could produce a sufficiently good thesis on a scientific subject.

Older, wiser and more experienced now, he didn't even try to be accepted as a regular student. He knew he would never be admitted to study there. Yet, according to those same strict university rules, it was possible for him to earn the degree if he could produce a "sufficiently good thesis on a scientific subject."

The two words, "sufficiently good," were the catch. Could he, with his patchwork education, with his transferring from school to school, present a "sufficiently good" enough thesis to win the highest of all academic degrees from the most difficult group of all to please? Would a committee of professors from the University of Zurich consider him good enough to wear the cap and gown of a Ph.D. from their university?

During that last year at the Polytechnic, he had worked under a professor of mechanics, Dr. Gustav Zeuner, who guided him through research on gases. In his work Wilhelm tried to find the characteristics of such gases as oxygen, nitrogen and air.

That research paper was almost finished:

Already in 1868, under the guidance of Dr. Gustav Zeuner, who was then professor of mechanics at the Polytechnic, I had completed an extensive work entitled, "Studies Concerning Gases" — a theme closely connected with my previous work and based on the theories of Clausius. This was the work which I now handed in to the philosophical faculty of the university, with a view to obtaining my Ph.D.

Mixed in with his feverish polishing of the details of his thesis in the spring of 1869 was his new-found sense of loneliness. Bertha was not in Zurich. She was not well, and her parents insisted that she move out of Zurich for a while until she recovered.

He knew where Bertha was recuperating. She was at Utelberg, a high, forested hill near Zurich. It was a favorite vacation spot for students. Bertha would do as she was told. She would stay there until her health improved.

But even though Utelberg was supposed to be for vacations and for fun, his Bertha soon found a way to earn many an extra franc while others only relaxed. She built up a small business by collecting wild flowers on the Utelberg and selling them to be made up in bouquets of dried flowers.

Wilhelm knew Bertha was just as anxious as he to learn the decision of the faculty of the University of Zurich.

The thesis was finished. He submitted it and waited. There was absolutely nothing he could do but wait. It was all out of his hands.

Once again he was being judged by a group of teachers. What would be their opinion this time? He could never forget how an earlier verdict of another group of teachers had almost cost him his whole education. What would happen to him now?

When the waiting became almost too much for him, they told him the faculty had reached a decision. Their verdict: his thesis was "sufficiently good."

The Ph.D. was his.

The words "sufficiently good" hung suspended in the air, surrounding him with a sense of well-being that he had never experienced before.

He had wanted the Ph.D. so much that he almost couldn't believe it was his at last. Now, and forever more, those three letters tacked after his name would speak for him.

One of the professors complimented him: "The work in question contains more than adequate proof of very sound knowledge and a gift for independent research in the field of mathematical physics."

In June 1869, he was awarded the Ph.D. from the University of Zurich. Now he was a true scientist in the eyes of the world.

The first and only person he could share that triumph with was Bertha. As he told about it years later:

When I received my doctor's diploma . . . I rushed to the Utelberg near Zurich, where my sweetheart was staying on account of her health, and we were very happy and proud, though the whole thing actually did not mean very much, and I had good reason to worry about an entirely uncertain future. I had two diplomas, one as an engineer and the other as a Ph.D.; however, I could not bring myself to go into practical engineering according to my original plan.

He couldn't help thinking back to the ten years of struggles to earn it, and of all the problems he had faced, all starting with the sketch on the fire screen. He couldn't help realizing, too, that with the highest degree of all in physics, he had gone to few lectures on the subject. What was more, he had never attended a complete course of lectures on experimental physics itself — the very subject which earned him his Ph.D.

8

Troubles with Parents

What do you do when you have earned the highest degree of all, and you still don't know what you want to do with your life?

As if that wasn't enough of a problem, Wilhelm knew the family, and most of all his father, didn't like the idea that he was going to marry Bertha Ludwig.

His parents had not yet met Bertha, but the elder Roentgen was not making a secret of his disappointment over the match. It seemed that his father had more ambitious plans for his only son. Shouldn't Wilhelm marry the daughter of a wealthy and well-known family, just as his father had?

Wilhelm knew that his mother's family had been prosperous and prominent in Holland, as had been his father's family in Rhineland. The elder Roentgen believed that his son and only heir should continue that custom and enter a good marriage.

Although her family was respected, Bertha was far from

wealthy. She was not bringing a large dowry into the marriage with her. Further, her father's inn could hardly be called an "excellent business," for he had almost nothing to give his middle daughter as a wedding present.

Whatever money he did have, Herr Ludwig had spent on her education at a girls' boarding school. Once, years earlier, in the fifties, her father had written:

Dear Bertha,

I do not want to lay aside the pen with which I have just written to your teacher without also writing you a few words. I am very happy to learn from Miss Grossmann that she is well satisfied with you in every respect. This shows that you appreciate the great sacrifice which your parents are happy to make for your education and that you are determined to contribute all you can to become what we would like you to be, sincere, orderly, and morally and scientifically well educated. These are the only treasures which you can acquire with the help of our efforts and those of your good teachers. Other treasures we cannot give to you, and even if we could, they truly would not be worth as much as these.

I was happy to read that you continue to feel well. You seem to like the climate and mode of life, which makes you long less for your parents' home. You may easily forget the pleasures which you shared with us. The weather continues to be bad and takes away all of the summer pleasures; it is probably the same in Neuchâtel. And now, my dear daughter, continue to be industrious and good, so that we may always receive good news of you. A very sincere good-bye from all of us.

Your loving father.

The summer before the engagement was a restless one. The cloud of his father's strong disapproval hung over them both, although Wilhelm was sure that as soon as his father met Bertha, he would change his mind about her.

Finally, it was October, and his parents arrived on a train from Apeldoorn. This was their first visit to Zurich since he had come there four years earlier. Their visit was something he had been wanting for a long time. He wanted to show the city of Zurich and the schools to his parents, but most important of all, he wanted them to meet Bertha and to give their consent to an engagement.

As it will happen after the first few minutes of being glad to see you, your parents will begin to ask questions. Then after the questions they begin to tell you what you should do, and what you have done that is wrong.

His parents, especially his father, were astonished, more than that, angry, to see how he had spent their "hard-earned money." Why and how could Wilhelm be so extravagant? To hire, often, and to drive a four-horse carriage through the streets of Zurich? His father thundered; he could not understand this wasteful spending of money. In no uncertain terms, both scolded, Wilhelm would have to be more careful and more mature about his spending. He was twenty-four and a half years old, he was not a seventeen-year-old student in the gymnasium at Utrecht. Surely by now Wilhelm should know the value of money.

But in spite of the scolding, they were pleased and proud. He was their only son and heir, and he had proven himself. He had earned the Ph.D., the highest degree a school could give, the most difficult.

They met Bertha and if the elder Roentgen did not like her, he kept his opinion to himself. He would not let the outside world know of his objections. In a letter to a friend, Mr. Buscher, in Lennep, on October 3, 1869, Roentgen's father wrote:

After we left Lennep, we continued our trip for three short days and arrived by railroad in Zurich, where we were greeted by our son. We were very happy to be with him and met a Zurich girl about whom Wilhelm had already written to us. We had not given a definite answer to his letters, but when he insisted on having our opinion, we considered it our parental duty to look into the matter, and were favorably impressed when we met her. Then we spent two weeks in Zurich, and decided that in order to get better acquainted with the girl, we would take her and Wilhelm to Baden-Baden for a few days and then to Wildbad for two weeks. The result was that when we said good-bye in Karlsruhe, for we were returning home, and they to Zurich, we gave our consent to the engagement. The girl (Bertha Ludwig) is well educated, comes from a good family, is intelligent, of good character, and very agreeable.

Wilhelm knew the custom of marriage in Apeldoorn: once accepted, the happy man had to go through certain steps. First of all, he exchanged rings, so that a man who was engaged or married betrayed the fact as well as a woman by a plain gold ring worn on the third finger of the left hand.

Then, the engagement was announced by sending out cards countersigned by both sets of parents. That was why it was important to obtain his parents' approval.

After that, a day was fixed for receiving the congratulations. The betrothed were then considered almost married. As a rule, engagements were not long, but in their case Wilhelm and Bertha were to wait for three more long years.

During that period, Bertha spent only part of her time in Zurich with him or with her own family. The rest of the time she spent in Apeldoorn with the older Roentgens. It was the custom for the bride-to-be to live with the groom's family and take cooking lessons from his mother. By the time they would marry, Wilhelm expected Bertha to have mastered his mother's way of cooking and to be able to prepare his meals just as his mother did. Mrs. Roentgen would also teach Bertha how to become a good, thrifty, Dutch housewife, to bargain with the tradesmen, to keep a well-scrubbed house and to manage a smoothly run household.

9

Beginning It All

He was beginning to change. He could sense that he was a different person in the laboratory now. There was less and less of the carefree student who once wore extravagant white suits to shock the townspeople and who fell in love with an actress. It was almost as if his interest in experimental physics was remolding him. For the first time in his life, he was being forced to reason, to doubt, and to analyze in a way he had never done before.

Much of the change in him was due to August Kundt, the professor who was daring enough to make different decisions about physics as the older scientists knew it. Kundt, at twenty-nine years, had already earned a reputation as a brilliant experimental physicist. He had come to the Polytechnic to succeed Professor Clausius, who had retired during Roentgen's last year there.

Professor Kundt was just five years older than Wilhelm, and just one year younger than Bertha. Roentgen knew that in the eyes of other scientists Kundt was young, very young. Perhaps it was because he was so very young that Kundt had the courage to pull away from all the older men's philosophies and theories about physics. Instead of just talking about science, as his elders did, August Kundt was performing experiments in laboratories — doing research.

What was more, he was adding many new demonstrations and experiments to the course of lectures on physics. In 1869 Professor Kundt had even organized an experimental laboratory course in physics for both the regular and advanced students. Although their laboratory had almost no equipment and was in a small room in the basement, it did give them a chance to study physics through experiments with machines and models instead of talking about it with pencil and paper.

This new idea, of experimenting to find an answer, was just what Roentgen wanted. At last he found something that interested him. Kundt had moved into this new field called experimental physics and Roentgen moved into it right along with his professor.

It would have been much easier for him to do the experiments if he could use both his eyes. He still had eye trouble. Not only was he colorblind, but he had good vision in only his right eye — the left one had been damaged by that illness he had just before coming to Zurich.

Then, after only a few semesters, in 1870, Kundt decided to accept a new post at the University of Würzburg in Bavaria. But before leaving, Professor Kundt asked Roentgen if he wanted to come to Würzburg with him. Without hesitating a second, he accepted the offer.

In Würzburg, Roentgen lived in the home of Mrs. Troll, who also owned a restaurant in Eckert's Garten in the

Veitshochheimer Strasse. The Physical Institute was in the building of the old university. The laboratory's windows looked out upon the Neubau Strasse, and he and Kundt liked, every now and then, to look across the street at some girls working in a tailor's shop and occasionally even to flirt with them.

Then, unexpectedly, he and Kundt found themselves arguing because Roentgen decided to go against Kundt's orders. Everyone knew that Kundt treasured his delicate instruments and would not allow anyone to touch them. These instruments were even kept separate from the other instruments, in a room which no one was permitted to enter.

But one Sunday afternoon, Roentgen decided he needed those delicate instruments for an experiment and used them. Professor Kundt, stopping at the laboratory, discovered him working in that forbidden room, using his private instruments and glassware. Now, for the second time in his life, Roentgen was in trouble with a teacher.

The older man lost his temper, but so did Roentgen. It was almost as if he were that schoolboy in Utrecht all over again. His fiery temper flared, and in a voice brimming with anger, he defended himself even though he had gone against the professor's orders.

Professor Kundt's reaction was mixed. Slowly, as he saw Roentgen's good intentions — only to work — and saw how carefully he handled the glassware and other tools, he excused him. But others at Würzburg did not think of Roentgen as being either that bright or that talented. And soon they would tell him so.

10

The Experimenter

It didn't take long for Roentgen to realize it. No one at the University of Würzburg thought he would make a good experimental scientist or teacher. What was even worse, they didn't waste any time in telling him.

It all came out soon after he and August Kundt began their new jobs at the university in 1870. Soon after they arrived, Professor Kundt, as his boss, asked the faculty to appoint Roentgen as a beginning teacher with the rank of *Privatdozent*. It was the lowest rank of all, barely that of an instructor, but it would mean that Roentgen would begin his career as a teacher.

The reason he was refused burned in Roentgen's mind for the rest of his life. Years later he told what happened: "Unfortunately, however, Würzburg University objected in principle to accepting anyone on their staff who had no *Matura*. At this my hopes of an academic career seemed to be sealed."

And they would have been to anyone less determined. But Professor Kundt wouldn't take no for an answer. If

47

Würzburg didn't think Wilhelm Roentgen was good enough to be a teacher, then August Kundt would find another school that would give his young friend a chance.

And so, the next term, Roentgen and his chief began another new position at the "newly founded Imperial German University in Strasbourg." The city of Strasbourg itself was the capital of the province of Alsace-Lorraine. This was the territory just won by the Germans in the bitter Franco-Prussian war:

In the aftermath of the victorious Franco-Prussian war, life was freer and many an ancient tradition had been cast aside. Kundt at once realized that here was a favorable opportunity for my graduation — a realization for which I can never be sufficiently grateful to him. Many another in his position would no longer have bothered himself about the future of his assistant, the less so after his first attempt to nominate me had been turned down. This time, in order to make double sure, he first obtained the support of two influential colleagues, and only then put his suggestion before the faculty. And: lo and behold. What Würzburg had vetoed but a few months previously, Strasbourg now accepted by a large majority. I finally received my diploma, and so began my academic career. A man must always have luck in life if he is to get anywhere.

The months passed, and it was now three years since Bertha and he had become engaged. With the steady income from the University of Strasbourg, they could be married at last.

They were finally married on January 19, 1872. Wilhelm was twenty-seven and Bertha was thirty-three. But even though they had known each other for all that time, those first months of marriage weren't easy.

They both were always worried about money. There was never enough. In the back of his mind, Wilhelm had counted on his father to help them by sending money regularly. But that plan fell through. His father, never really happy over their marriage, still grumbled about Bertha. Now he showed his disapproval by not sending them any money. Without those extra funds, Roentgen and Bertha didn't really have enough to live on.

Of the two, he knew he was the one who was finding it the most difficult to live on very little. He simply wasn't used to worrying about money or finding he didn't have enough to pay his bills. Of course, his wife was doing more than her share to help out.

Bertha did all of her own cooking, washing, sewing and mending, and he knew her life was not especially easy. In spite of all she did to make it comfortable, he found their home, a little house on Heidingsfeler Strasse, small and somewhat plain. He had been used to the much more beautiful and comfortable homes of his parents and of his university years.

Not only didn't he like the struggle over money, he didn't like it when Bertha disagreed with him. He was used to having his own way. If he didn't get it, he lost his temper, and then there was a quarrel. Once, in the midst of a fight, he completely lost his temper about money. It happened when he and Bertha took a walk on the Frankenwarte. While they were angrily disagreeing, he stopped a coachman who happened to pass by, put his wife into the carriage, gave the coachman his fare and their address, and continued his walk alone.

His excitable temperament, his high words, hot blood and black looks whenever he was angry, was something he never did learn to control. Eventually he saw Bertha was growing used to his fits of temper and learned that she did not hold a grudge.

By the next year he knew they would have to move on. Although they loved their friends at Strasbourg, and he enjoyed the work at the university, he was ready for a more important teaching post. Most of all, they desperately needed the higher salary it would bring.

On April 1, 1875, he joined the faculty at the Agricultural Academy at Hohenheim as the new professor of mathematics and physics.

But almost as soon as they moved to Hohenheim they knew it was a mistake.

It didn't take him and Bertha long to discover that no matter how much money he was earning, they never should have left Strasbourg. Everything at Hohenheim was wrong. They didn't like the people, they missed their friends. Even more important to Roentgen was the poor condition of the equipment the university gave him to work with. It was almost useless, unfit to use in experiments.

As they considered it, the only thing Strasbourg and Hohenheim had in common was that he and Bertha had to fight off household pests in both places.

In Hohenheim there were rats in our house, and we were on very friendly terms with them. They got their daily food from the garbage in the kitchen sink. Aside from that they didn't disturb us. In our apartment in Strasbourg we found bedbugs and cockroaches, but my wife soon exterminated them.

Once again Kundt rescued them.

In 1876, after a year and a half of being exiles, Kundt offered Roentgen another job at Strasbourg. But now he would return there as an associate professor of physics. He was promoted from the rank of lowly instructor at last.

For the next three years Roentgen worked on different research projects in different fields of physics. It was still the same with him. Just as he never wanted to be pinned down when he was younger, he still didn't want to be pinned down to just one kind of research.

In those three years he wrote fifteen different papers on his research which were published in a magazine, *Annalen der Physik und Chemie.*

The first batch of papers concerned experiments on the specific heats of gases. Then he switched to a completely different kind of physics, writing a paper about "On soldering platinum-plated glasses"; still later he described a telephonic alarm in 1878, and then a new instrument for measuring atmospheric pressure, called an aneroid barometer. There were more papers: on discharges of electricity under various conditions and on the conductivity of heat in crystals, on the effect of pressure on liquids, how water vapor soaks up heat, the thickness of oil film on water, what water is made up of, and still more.

Of all these different experiments, he found he was

most interested in crystals. All the laws of nature, it seemed to him, were summed up in crystals, and he wanted to find out as much as he could about them.

It all didn't happen at once. It had been building little by little, but he could tell that now other scientists at other schools were beginning to notice his work. At last, three years later, in 1879, he was offered an important new post. He was invited to become Professor of Physics at the University of Giessen.

The invitation meant much more than just another new position. It meant that he was being accepted at last by the important scientists. The best-known physicists of Germany, von Helmholtz, Kirchhoff, Meyer, and others had suggested Roentgen for the post, even though he was only thirty-four. Of course he accepted.

With this new appointment came a grand new title: Professor of Physics and Director of the Physical Institute of the Ludwigs University in Giessen.

And so he and Bertha moved again.

But when they arrived, Roentgen could barely hide his disappointment. The lecture room and the physics laboratory were in their house on the Frankfurter Strasse. That is, he was to hold lectures and have his laboratories on the first floor of his home, and he and Bertha would live upstairs. Whatever equipment he found at Giessen did not compare with the instruments he left behind with Kundt at Strasbourg.

He may have changed to a new school, and he may have had a new title, but it always seemed the same for him. Wherever he went, he was always finding something that he wanted to change because he believed it had to be better.

While he was working at the laboratories, he knew Bertha was doing her part to help make new friends in the new city. In almost no time they found people whom they liked. There was Professor and Mrs. von Hippel; the surgeon Kronlein; Gaffky; the Hofmeires; Gareis; the zoologist, Theodor Boveri, his wife Margaret and their daughter, and even more.

For the first time, they could afford to rent a vacation house. Now Roentgen could spend more time on hunting. Much as he loved his work, he couldn't wait to spend the spring holidays on the Rhine and to wander in the countryside around Giessen.

Life should have been pleasant for them both. Certainly it was so for him, but he couldn't help noticing that Bertha did not seem as content as he. It was easy to understand why. It was seven years now since they had been married, and they had no children. Yet Bertha loved them; he did too. In spite of all the interesting work at the laboratory, in spite of all their good friends and good life, he, too, would have liked children.

It was Bertha's brother who helped them. He sent his six-year-old daughter from Zurich to Giessen to live with them. His child, Josephine Bertha Ludwig, had been born in Zurich on December 21, 1881. He would allow the Roentgens to bring her up as their own.

And so it was that, at Giessen, they not only found life-long friends, but they became parents, too.

Now that little Bertha was living with them, life was

peppered with disagreements. The only real quarrels he and Bertha seemed to have were over little Bertha, especially her education. When it came to her learning, he thought his wife allowed the child too much freedom. On the other hand, he knew his wife thought him too strict with her.

For instance, he had small patience with little Bertha when she complained that she was too sick to go to school. As a matter of fact, she was sickly so often that she could not attend school regularly, and stayed home more than she attended classes. As far as Roentgen was concerned, he thought that the child's continual sickliness was only made worse when his wife pampered her and allowed her to stay home.

Someone had to be somewhat strict with little Bertha. He insisted that she get up early in the morning, tidy up her own room, and learn one new lesson, such as language or music, very thoroughly each day.

As she grew older and became more and more interested in boys, he insisted on some other rules for his daughter. He didn't approve of the young girl's becoming acquainted with the students at the dueling clubs or fraternities of the university. He also forbade his daughter to stroll in the streets of their small university district so as to see and be seen by the students. Once he gave her an order, he expected her to obey him without any further discussion. And that was that.

For the most part, though, life at Giessen was taking on a pleasant pattern for the three of them. They went south for winter vacations; then, in the spring, they went to the lakes of northern Italy, where they celebrated his and his wife's birthday. In the fall, before going to the Alps, they all spent two weeks at someplace in Switzerland at a lower altitude, perhaps Rigi-Scheidegg or Lenzerheide, and after that went up to the Engadine Mountains, where he climbed, played cards, and helped his wife collect her beloved wild flowers.

Roentgen remained at Giessen until he was forty-three. While he was there he wrote nineteen papers. Almost all of those nineteen papers were each on a different field of physics. After all this time, he still didn't like to stay with any one kind of research for very long.

It was habit now, when a study was finished, to quickly transfer his interest to something else. After he explored one thing for a while, he would leave it and begin to investigate a completely new question about nature.

Yet, as much as he enjoyed wandering about in his research, he kept coming back to the study of crystals. He was fascinated by the effect of temperature on crystals — in the electrified state in some crystals produced by and changing with temperature. It was called the pyro and piezo electrical phenomena in crystals. But he was also interested in the effect of pressure on different kinds of substances. Then he started a series of investigations on how water soaks up heat.

Almost without realizing it, somehow along the way, he had shed many of the habits he had years earlier as a student. For instance, he no longer had that "I don't care" attitude about money. Even so, he could still remember how he enjoyed spending money when he was younger, and doing it whenever it pleased him.

Now, fifteen years later, he was spending money only when he was sure it was absolutely necessary. He had to be sure he was getting the full worth. This was especially true when spending the government's money for the laboratory. If the government trusted him enough to give him money to run his laboratory, to pay for the equipment, salaries and other expenses, he must show them he was worthy of their trust.

He took especial care to manage the money efficiently; it was his duty to save as much as possible. He didn't give it a second thought if his thriftiness made it all the more difficult for his students and assistants; he wanted them to know he would not tolerate wastefulness or extravagance.

The years as a professor had seasoned him and changed his outlook. Instead of being extravagant and easygoing, he was now known — to his friends and fellow scientists — as a man who hated to waste either time or money.

Instead of being unsure of himself as he once was, he was always certain of what he wanted from the world. In a large measure he was doing almost exactly what he wanted to — and if he was working longer and harder than others, it was only because that was the way he wanted it to be. Each day he had more and more positions open to him. The days when he couldn't get a job as a beginning instructor seemed to belong to another world or to someone else.

Within a few years he received offers from two more universities. In 1886 he received an offer from the University of Jena, a city in east Germany. The offer meant little to him and he refused it.

But then, in 1888, Roentgen finally had a chance to refuse the same people who more than twenty years earlier would not allow him to enter their school. He could remember all too well what it meant to be told by the University of Utrecht that he could not attend classes there. He was not qualified because he did not have the *Matura*. But now he was being offered a position at Utrecht because of the "excellent quality of his publications, which show an exceptional intellect and profound knowledge combined with originality of ideas." He, himself, was told he was also "a brilliant teacher of great experimental skill." If he could only have known this in the early years when he could not get into the University of Utrecht! Now the tables were turned and he had a chance to say "no" to the same school that had earlier made his life so miserable for so long.

Much as he wanted to say more when refusing them, he wrote only a polite note to the University of Utrecht: "To move into entirely new surroundings would require too much of my time, which I had rather devote to scientific investigations."

And then, on October 1, 1888, still another school that years earlier also had been unwilling to accept him, offered him a position. Eighteen years earlier, the University of Würzburg refused to hire him at the lowest rank of all, as instructor on their faculty. Now, that same school was inviting him to become head of their new, important institute, the new Physical Institute at Würzburg.

If he accepted their offer, he would return to the University of Würzburg as a respected scientist and outstanding professor. He would be replacing an older man, the well-known experimental physicist, Friedrich Kohlrausch, who was going to teach at the University of Strasbourg. He was being offered Kohlrausch's post because both were known as experimenters. And now they thought he was outstanding enough to replace Kohlrausch.

He could never forget how, in spite of all of August Kundt's pleading eighteen years earlier, the faculty at the University of Würzburg had decided he was not good enough to teach there. It had taken years, but now he was being invited to return to that same place as a person of importance. This was the dream of anyone who was ever refused because he was "not good enough." He still had not completed the usual high school course; he still did not have his *Matura* and all the qualifications they had insisted on earlier. Yet, now he was "good enough" to be offered the highest position of all in the very same department that once had told him they did not want him for the lowest of all teaching posts.

It didn't take him long to decide. Of course he would accept the offer from Würzburg. Perhaps by being at Würzburg, he would be a reminder to those who judged him earlier as "unfit." Sometimes someone who does not go along strictly with each rule of a school system can also be successful in later life.

11

Würzburg
Changes Its Mind

Roentgen didn't like to leave any loose ends. It had taken years to build up the physics department at Giessen. Now he wanted to be sure he was leaving it in good hands. His friend Heinrich Rudolph Hertz, the German physicist, would be the best replacement. And so Hertz was offered the position he was leaving.

His friend was as precise in asking questions about Giessen as he was in doing experiments. Hertz even thought of how long it would take Roentgen to reply to the questions he was asking. To save them both time, Hertz sent him a questionnaire to fill out.

Snatching time from his schedule on September 27, 1888, Roentgen replied:

I am briefly answering your letter, which I have just received, because I must go out of town this afternoon until tomorrow morning, and I therefore use your suggestion by answering the questionnaire which you sent.

ROENTGEN'S REVOLUTION

A. In regard to teaching:
   (1) I lectured on experimental physics five hours per week during both semesters; I gave no other lecture courses.
   (2) The practical exercises took two afternoons per week from two until five o'clock if the number of students was less than eight, otherwise they took four afternoons.
   (3) The number of students attending the main lecture was around seventy; usually it was somewhat larger.
   (4) The number of students in the practical courses has decreased somewhat during the last few years, probably because the outlook is gloomy for the future of natural scientists and mathematicians. The highest number was twenty-three and the lowest six (during the last semester).
   (5) On the whole, the students are very industrious.
   (6) The associate professor lectured on theoretical physics. The employees of the institute are first an assistant at a salary of one thousand marks [about two hundred and thirty American dollars], and the diener at a salary of one thousand marks, free apartment in the building with light and heat.
   (7) The yearly budget for operating the institute is two thousand two hundred and fifty marks. Heat and light are paid from a special fund of the university.
   (8) As a director of the Mathematical-Physical Cabinet and the Goedetic Institute, the associate professor has over six hundred marks per year at his disposal.
B. In regard to income:
   (1) The minimum salary is four thousand marks; I received five thousand marks when I came here.
   (2) During the last few years, I have received a salary of fifty-five hundred marks. (As far as I know, there are no special funds for housing).

(3) and (4) The income from lectures and examinations amounted to about fifty-five hundred marks per year.

(5) I shall obtain information about pensions and communicate with you later.

C. In regard to the city:

(1) An apartment of five to six large rooms costs from nine hundred to one thousand marks, according to the location. I pay seventeen hundred marks for my apartment containing nine rooms and in the best location with a beautiful garden.

(2) Living conditions are moderate; Strasbourg was decidedly more expensive.

(3) City taxes are not particularly high; I shall write about them to you later.

(4) and (5) At present I know of no important advantages or disadvantages.

D. I enclose the pamphlets requested.

E. Could be answered better in person but need not make you suspicious. In this connection I thought of the statement in Baedeker's *Rhineland*: "Giessen . . . seat of a University with old established institutions and equipment." But this is really not true.

F. Building a separate institute would be a very important improvement. This is entirely within the realm of possibility because, first, it was contemplated several years ago, and second, it receives the support of the colleagues who lecture in our building because they are often disturbed by the work in the Physical Institute (gas, motor, et cetera), and finally, the present rooms (especially the lecture and equipment rooms) are entirely inadequate. I think, however, that it is not a favorable time at present to insist upon a new building, but only to suggest it. The authorities have been asked for large sums for building a clinic and for the pathological and chemical institutes.

61

During the nine years that I have been here, I have had the experience several times of finding that we can get considerable from the government of Hessen; however, it takes time.

I hope that we can get you to come to Giessen. I must close now and will always be glad to give you more information.

Roentgen to H. Hertz, Giessen, September 27, 1888

It no longer mattered to Roentgen what others thought of him or how they judged him. All that mattered was that he be free to do whatever work he wanted. And when his research finally forced a new fact from nature, he enjoyed a sense of freedom that was beyond words.

He tried to share his feelings about research with his students, in a lecture he gave, by quoting from the memoirs of Werner von Siemens, the British inventor who had been born in Germany:

If the key to a long-sought mechanical combination has been found, if the missing link of a chain of thought is fortuitously supplied, this then gives to the discoverer the exultant feeling that comes with victory of the mind which alone can compensate him for all the struggle and effort; and which lifts him to a higher plane of existence.

Roentgen knew one of the main reasons he had been asked to come to Würzburg. He was famous now for being able to design new instruments which could measure extremely small effects in research experiments. Until now, that was considered almost impossible to do by the other researchers. But for him, designing simple equipment was easy because that was how he thought about experiments.

Any good experiment, he believed, should be kept as simple as possible. He didn't use higher mathematics or complicated calculations in working out his ideas. But before he began an experiment he would first work it all out on paper, using mathematics. Whenever he did the calculations, he was able to "see" in his mind's eye what the numbers would mean when he built the equipment and ran the tests. Sometimes he would advise a student: "The physicist, in preparing for his work, needs three things, mathematics, mathematics, and mathematics."

As always, he built much of his equipment by himself. It was a habit still carried from his school days at Apeldoorn. He could still remember how he built those little mechanical gadgets when he was a schoolboy. Now he built instruments to tell about some of the most complicated facts in nature.

He liked to work all by himself. He knew he was supposed to have a mechanic to help him, but one always made him feel uncomfortable. He used an assistant only when he absolutely had to. It was only when he needed another person to help him build a complicated piece of equipment, or when he needed someone to observe him as he became part of an experiment, or when he knew he would have trouble because of his green colorblindness, that he would allow an assistant to help him around the laboratory.

By accepting the position at Würzburg, Roentgen

knew he was now forever linked in a chain of world-famous scientists. He was now considered one of the best. Yet, in spite of his new, important position at Würzburg, he knew he would still be as independent as before. He would not change his thinking about Würzburg, but now Würzburg would have to change its thinking about him.

12

The Good Life

Moving to Würzburg meant that the family would be living in the heart of Franconia, at a crossroads marking where north and south Bavaria met. The city, nestled in a hollow as if in the center of a huge saucer, was filled with chapels and castles. All were overdecorated with beautiful statues of the Madonna or of a saint.

Würzburg had its age-old customs and traditions. One of them was the yearly wine festival, another was the University of Würzburg. Begun in 1582, the university was now over three hundred years old. It was one of the most important scientific centers in Bavaria.

Although the university buildings were scattered all over Würzburg, the Physical Institute, where Wilhelm would teach, was in the center of the city. It was on a street facing a park called the Pleicher Ring.

The institute was a square, plain, brick building planned for sensible work. There was no resemblance to the delicately carved and decorated chapels and castles which made Würzburg famous.

One day it would be a world-famous landmark, but in 1888 there was nothing unusual about the building. It had a basement and two upper floors. The square windows of the basement level were at street height and were spaced directly under the square windows of the first floor, which were directly under the square windows of the second floor.

The only unusual part of the building was the topmost floor because it had a glassed-in conservatory where Bertha could grow her flowers and plants.

Both his research and his family were all together in the same building again. Their own apartment was on the top floor. By walking downstairs to the lower floors Roentgen was in the classrooms, laboratories and offices of the Physical Institute.

In almost no time, the three of them settled down to a professor's life in a university town. Life is different, Roentgen knew, when people want you and need you, than when you want and need them. He couldn't help but remember how cold and unfriendly the city of Würzburg seemed eighteen years earlier. This time it was altogether different.

As "Herr Professor," he was now treated with respect. His wife, called "Frau Professor," and daughter, too, were treated as people of importance. Whatever they wanted to do, wherever they went, all three were welcome.

He and Bertha particularly enjoyed the rich and lavish dinners of many courses given by the medical professors. They loved all the good food, particularly the little white fish, the *graubrot* or gray or brown bread, the veal and potatoes, the dumplings, the Camembert cheese, and always the famous Franken wine, which came from the vineyards around Würzburg.

They quickly found a circle of interesting friends and joined a group, the Club of Youth, which staged little plays and costumed dances. Sometimes Roentgen and Bertha and the other members used to noisily parade home through the gaslit cobblestone streets carrying Japanese lanterns. He even discovered he was something of a poet. He took pleasure in writing yearly reports for the club, which he made up in rhyme, mocking the members and nonmembers for their odd traits and peculiarities.

Once again life slipped into a pleasant pattern, just as it had in Giessen. He had his freedom to do research, his teaching, his friends and clubs, a family who wanted only to please him. After all, what more could any man want?

And yet, even though he seemed to be at ease with life, there was still that streak of independence and a temper which could quickly explode at the slightest excuse.

This was particularly true if he thought someone was mistreating Bertha, just as happened once at a dinner party. Like so many of the other professors and their wives, he and Bertha loved to be invited for dinner by the royalty of Franconia or by the high army officers stationed in Würzburg. The evening he had lost his temper, he and Bertha were having dinner at the home of a well-known nobleman. When dinner was announced, he noticed that all the ladies of royalty had professors assigned to

67

them as dinner partners, but the wives of the professors were left to shift for themselves. As soon as he saw what was happening, Roentgen left a countess who had been assigned to him and took his own wife in to dinner.

Another time, others wanted to tear up the university botanical gardens. The university wanted to build a new building where the gardens were located. Losing little time, Roentgen organized his friends Prym and Boveri as a committee to protest the action. They managed to stop the project long enough to bring it to a vote before the faculty.

That same pride and independence now were winning respect from his fellow workers, too. After six years there, in 1894, Roentgen was promoted to rector of the University of Würzburg. Now he was to head the same school that had once refused to hire him as a teacher.

There were impressive ceremonies making him rector. In his speech that day he told the audience:

The university is a nursery of scientific research and mental education, a place for the cultivation of ideals for students as well as for teachers. . . . Teachers and students of the university should consider it a great honor to be members of this organization. Pride in one's profession is demanded, but not professional conceit, snobbery or academic arrogance, all of which grow from false egotism. One should feel strongly that one belongs to a favored profession which gives many rights but also requires many duties.

Did some of the listeners move uneasily in their seats? Perhaps they were the same ones who years earlier had decided that he was not good enough for the lowest teaching position of all at Würzburg. It seemed that no matter how successful he would become, Roentgen would never forget those terrible years when no one wanted him because he did not get the usual kind of education and fulfill the usual kind of requirements.

Even now, he was once again fighting for a different way of doing something. He wanted the world to understand how important experiments were to science. Right now, only a few scientists were willing to do research. The rest of them still only talked about science. They still explained everything in nature with pencil and paper — as theories. Most of them never dreamed of testing their ideas to see if they would work.

Of course, they still needed people with ideas, but now science had grown to need people who also performed with instruments. In that same speech Roentgen told the students and faculty gathered to honor him why he was an experimenter:

Only gradually has the conviction gained importance that the experiment is the most powerful and the most reliable lever enabling us to extract secrets from nature, and that the experiment must constitute the final judgment as to whether a hypothesis should be retained or be discarded.

The modern experiments he was talking about now were far different from the ones of the ancient alchemists who kept trying to change stones into gold. Those old-fashioned experimenters had insisted that there was something mysterious and unseen in nature. But the modern experimenters of 1894 no longer believed in anything invisible. They tested and worked only with what they could see, feel, or touch. The years of thinking that there was something hidden and unknown in nature were now gone from science.

Yet, there were many who still didn't agree with Roentgen's new ideas about research. That was why he had to be sure everything he did, everything his students did, everything that came from his laboratory, was always absolutely perfect. Everything, he insisted, had to be read by him first before it could be sent out as news for others to read and to criticize.

Once, when a student dared to send out a report without showing it to him first, he wasted no time in writing to the scientific journal *Physikalische Zeitschrit*: "This communication was not submitted to me before its publication and I gave no permission to the signature."

These days he had little patience for anyone who seemed lazy. If a student didn't study he couldn't stay. That meant no student could remain if he could not make good grades on his examinations. He knew his exams were famous for being strict and severe. He was careful to make up questions which tested each student's scientific keenness.

Yet, there would always be a part of him remembering exams as unfair. Someday he would write:

Students' examinations usually do not give an indication of the capacity for a subject but unfortunately they are a necessary evil. Oh, those examinations! They are needed to keep

70

many a student from a profession for which he would be too lazy or too unskilled, and they don't always even perform that function. At any rate, they are a torture for both parties, the recollection of which causes nightmares even in later years. The experience of life itself is the real test of capacity for any kind of profession.

13

X Rays

Up to the end of 1894 Roentgen had written less than fifty papers about his experiments. It was not a lot, considering that they covered twenty-five years of research either alone or with someone else. He wrote the first one in Zurich, back in 1869, fifteen while at Strasbourg, only one at Hohenheim, but nineteen at Giessen and the rest while at Würzburg.

Even after writing for a quarter of a century he still didn't like to put anything down on paper. Partly he was afraid to put his findings into print. What if he had made an error? Once it was published, if there was a mistake somewhere in his experiment, he could no longer correct it. And, partly, he could not write well. He would rather show something with an experiment than tell about it. It was far easier, when he finished a set of experiments, to quickly become interested in a newer problem without taking the time to write about the research just over with.

But even though he didn't write as much as other scientists, he knew his experiments in many different areas of physics were well known all over the world. He was famous now for building simple equipment to accurately measure the very small changes in physics which no one had been able to measure before.

He had even been able to perform some experiments to prove a twenty-year-old theory of British physicist James Clerk Maxwell. In 1873 Maxwell had published his famous equations in his book, *Treatise on Electricity and Magnetism*. Only Roentgen had been able to build the equipment to test Maxwell's ideas.

By the fall of 1896 Roentgen's students weren't especially surprised to learn that he was going to study still another part of physics. Electricity was just being developed and he wanted to learn more about it. By this time, scientists had learned not only how to begin to harness the power of steam, but they were well on their way to learning how to use something new, called "electricity." Just as with steam, electricity was being used without completely understanding its invisible power.

Interested scientists investigated electricity and learned that it was made up of tiny bits, all the same, carrying what they called a "negative charge." About twenty years earlier, in 1874, the Irish physicist Stoney, named these bits "electrons." If a large enough number of these electrons settled on something, it was said to be electrically charged.

The electron itself was discovered in a tube, but not the kind that the chemists used. It was discovered in the kind of tube that, over one hundred and fifty years later, would develop into something called the radio tube and the TV tube. Today's TV sets carry a part, the "electron tube," named after those first tubes.

But the tubes of Roentgen's day were much less complicated than the tubes of today. Then, they were just a piece of glass pipe closed at both ends. Inside the pipe, there were just two metal wires sealed into each end of each tube. When the electrons traveled along the wires, the path they made was called an electrical current.

As they worked, physicists learned that the air between the two wires in the tube kept the electrons traveling along each wire, and away from the electrons traveling along the other wire. The air was used as something called insulation. With a lot of air, there was a lot of insulation and little or no electrical charge.

Soon the physicists began to pump air out of the tube to see what would happen. As they did, the air inside the tube became thinner and thinner and there was less and less insulation between the wires. At the same time the air grew thinner and thinner, streaks of soft shades of red and purple light began to glimmer along the wires. Then, as more and more air was pumped out of the tube, the reddish-purple glow grew dimmer and dimmer. Finally, it disappeared.

The tubes, with the air pumped out of them, were called by a new name: vacuum tubes. A vacuum was a space that had nothing at all in it: no air, or gas, or water, or anything. A vacuum tube was a glass tube that had almost all the air pumped out of it. The wires sealed in at both ends were named the anode and the cathode. A cathode ray was made up of a stream of electrons coming from the cathode. Some of the tubes were later called cathode-ray tubes because of that stream of electrons coming from the cathode.

Two German physicists, Hittorff and Schuster, and an English physicist, Sir William Crookes, had been working with those special tubes. They all found that, as rays traveled across the empty vacuum tube and hit the opposite wall, they caused the glass wall of the vacuum tube to shine with an eerie greenish-blue light. Also, if they put something inside the tube in the path of these rays, the objects cast a shadow on the walls of the tube.

Still later, they found that if a magnet was held close to the vacuum tube, the rays traveling inside could be forced to change direction. To the scientists, this meant that the newly discovered rays were not ordinary light rays, and that probably they carried a negative charge of electricity.

At first, Sir William Crookes called these rays "radiant matter," but later scientists called them by the name Stoney had already chosen, "electrons."

On that Friday evening in 1895, Roentgen was experimenting with that eerie greenish-blue light produced by the electron rays. He was using the vacuum tube and a gadget called a "Crookes Tube," designed by Sir William Crookes.

Now he was applying a powerful current of electricity to a pear-shaped Crookes tube. Earlier that fall, he had begun this investigation by using some of the results of

Philipp Lenard, another scientist. By November, he had moved on to his own thinking and his own way of working.

That Friday evening, November 8, 1895, everyone else, including his assistant, had long since gone home. He was working alone as usual. He had made the laboratory as dark as possible to help his weakened eyes. Only if there was absolute black could he see what was going to happen.

This time he had wrapped the Crookes tube in a shield of black cardboard. Although scientists had already found that cathode rays could travel in straight lines and move through very thin sheets of metal, Roentgen was testing to find out more about them. How strong were they? Were they strong enough to travel through glass?

Roentgen would know whether or not the cathode rays could pass through glass by observing what happened outside the walls of the Crookes tube. From earlier experiments, he knew that as cathode rays came in contact with air, they caused a glow of color to appear. If the cathode rays in his experiment did manage to travel through the glass wall, a glow of color would spread around the outside of the Crookes tube. That glow then would be his clue telling him that cathode rays were strong enough to travel through glass.

As he turned on the electrical current, he could hear the crackling of the wires and smell the peculiar odor — like weak chlorine — of the ozone that came from the electrical discharges.

He sat and waited and watched.

Moments passed.

Straining to see, he carefully inspected the outside walls of the covered tube.

More time passed.

Still no glow.

At last he was convinced.

He had found out something new about cathode rays: they were not strong enough to travel through glass.

Satisfied that the test was over, he began to reach for the switch, meaning to turn off the electrical current.

Then he noticed a glow coming from a bench near his equipment.

Straining in the darkness to be certain that his eyes were not playing tricks on him, he peered over at that faint flickering light. The glow was coming from a piece of paper used for a completely different experiment. It had been left lying carelessly on a bench. What was interesting was that the paper had been treated with crystals of a chemical, barium platinocyanide.

There was absolutely no light in the laboratory, and nothing giving off any light. Nothing, that is, except the Crookes tube — but that was still wrapped in its black shield.

Moving the piece of paper closer to the tube, Roentgen saw that faint glow grow brighter. Moving it away from the tube, he saw the crystals' glow grow fainter, but not disappear.

Then he turned off the current. This time the glow

disappeared from the paper. Somehow, the cathode tube was affecting the barium-covered paper.

Reaching in the darkness for his notebook he wrote: "This is a new kind of invisible light. It is clearly new, something unrecorded."

Testing some more, he picked up a thick book of about one thousand pages someone left lying on a table. Holding it between the covered tube and the paper coated with barium, he looked over at the crystals. If the book were in front of ordinary light waves, it would have blocked out or soaked up the light. But even though he was holding the thick book in front of the covered tube, the crystals on the bench still gleamed, although not as brightly. Testing again, he replaced the book with a double pack of cards, then a single sheet of tinfoil, a thick block of wood, some pine boards, sheets of hard rubber, glass plates, water and other liquids — in fact, anything he could find. Still the crystals kept giving off a glow.

In all his years of experimenting he had never known anything like this. Alone, in that blackened laboratory, he knew he had to search out something invisible and unknown.

He knew absolutely nothing about those rays. He would call them "X rays," he decided. The X would stand for unknown. He sensed that here was something new, something never before explained in science. The current from the inside of the Crookes tube was sending off rays which in some mysterious way were keeping those crystals glowing.

It was much, much later than usual when he climbed the stairs to their apartment that night. He could see Bertha, still waiting up for him, was worried. What had happened at the laboratory to keep him so late?

"Oh nothing to worry about," he soothed her. "I was simply held up in the institute by a rather unusual discovery. Well, now, let the devil do his worst."

14

The Search

Nothing could keep him from his search. He needed now to blot out the rest of the world — students, scientists, friends, his daughter and even Bertha. He needed to be left alone to hunt for those unknown rays.

And so, he moved downstairs to live in his laboratory. No one could bother him there. He could concentrate on his work. He wouldn't have to keep track of day or night, to worry about being on time for meals, or to make explanations to anyone.

But he would not begin any tests until first he made sure that his equipment was working exactly as it should. After the instruments were checked out, he then repeated the tests of others who had also worked with cathode rays.

No one was allowed in his laboratory. He worked completely alone. He would not tell his assistants what he was working on. They were told to do their research somewhere else. For that matter, he would not even tell

Bertha. Somehow, something inside him insisted that he tell no one. Only once, not able to help himself, he told his best friend, the zoologist Theodor Boveri: "I have discovered something interesting but I do not know whether or not my observations are correct."

As Roentgen worked, he tried to do everything that would speed up his search. Although the windows of his laboratory were draped with heavy curtains and shades, he didn't want to have to take the time to close them each time he experimented. Even if he did close them, he was not satisfied that all daylight, or any light, was shut out of the room. He would only be satisfied that he had complete darkness if he built a small darkroom right inside his laboratory.

The darkroom he built was really a cabinet, about the size of a large packing crate. It was about seven feet high and four feet square with sheet-metal walls of zinc. Cutting into one side of the zinc-walled cabinet, he set in a round aluminum sheet about one-twenty-fifth of an inch thick and about eighteen inches in diameter. Those new rays would pass through this hole. He cut a zinc door on the other side of the booth — just opposite the aluminum disk — so that he could enter and leave the darkroom. Now he wouldn't waste any more time before an experiment. Whenever he wanted to go to work, all he had to do was to turn on the current, go into the darkroom, and close the door behind him.

Day blended into night and he lost count of them both. Although he was always a careful researcher, he knew that he must not overlook anything this time. Each time he experimented, he carefully repeated each step of it over and over again. He never did anything without first checking every part of his equipment to be sure that it was working as it should. Out of everything he tested, only two metals would stop the rays traveling from the cathode tube; they were lead and platinum.

One day he decided to test the strength of X rays on photographic plates. By looking at the photographic plates he could find out even more about the cathode rays.

Roentgen replaced the crystals with a photographic plate. Then he held something between the tube and the plate to take a picture. In that way he used X rays as a source of light. If the X rays were only as powerful as ordinary light rays, nothing would show up on the plate. He decided to photograph his brass house key. If X rays were indeed stronger than light rays, then he would have a photograph of the key.

Using an unexposed plate, Roentgen wrapped it in black paper to keep out ordinary light. Then, taking his brass house key, he placed it on the dark paper and put the wrapped-up film near the Crookes tube. Finally, he sent an electric current through the tube.

As soon as he could, he developed the plate and inspected it. Everything was all black except where he had placed the key. In fact, all he could see was the outline of that key. All at once he realized what it was. He was staring at the blurred outlines of his key's X-ray shadow.

Somehow those rays could travel in a way that no ordinary light waves could. He found different things around the laboratory — small metal weights of platinum, brass, aluminum, glasses, a coil of fine wire, a wooden spool. Then he took X-ray pictures of them all. After he developed the film he saw that the X rays had traveled through some objects and not others. When the X rays were stopped, whatever stopped them cast its shadowy outline on the exposed plate. He realized that it was just the same as when ordinary light rays are stopped by something; it also casts a shadow.

But what about humans, he wondered. What would happen if X rays were sent through people? Would X rays travel through humans just as they did through paper, wood, or glass?

The only way to find out was to experiment. He would use himself as the subject. Taking a small, short-legged bench from the laboratory, he painted it black. Then he put the bench on top of one of the larger tables in the laboratory. He put the Crookes tube a few inches from the underside of the table. Then he placed his hand flat on top of the stand and put a photographic plate over it. Stretching, he reached the light switch, turned off all the lights in the laboratory, and turned on the current in the Crookes tube.

After he developed the plate, it took him a while to realize what he was staring at. Here was something completely different, completely new. Instead of a photograph of his hand, he saw his bones and a silhouette of his thick gold wedding band. Those X rays had gone through his flesh, his muscles, his blood vessels, until they were stopped only by his bones. He was staring at the very first photograph of the inside of the human body.

15

Unnoticed

Like all researchers, Roentgen was always looking and hoping for a chance to make a new discovery in science. Now that he had made one, he wanted to be the first to tell the world about X rays. The announcement needed to be made quickly.

It was the custom among the scientists that credit for a new scientific discovery was always given to the first person who wrote about it in a magazine. Roentgen knew he must find a magazine that would publish his findings as soon as possible. It happened all too often that the same discovery might be made by different scientists working in different laboratories at opposite ends of the world.

Perhaps there was someone even now who had also found the X rays. With so many other scientists working on electricity, perhaps one had stumbled on X rays just as he had. With so many men searching out the science of electricity, it was a real possibility, a real danger. And seven weeks had already gone by.

He must find a scientific magazine that would quickly print his findings. A man of his position would be expected to send an announcement of this importance to the leading German scientific magazine in physics, the *Annalen der Physik und Chemie*, which had a worldwide circulation. But he knew they could not print it right away.

There was another, a local scientific journal, the magazine of the small Physico-Medical Society of Würzburg. It wasn't a well-known or widely read magazine. But it didn't matter. All that mattered was that it print his news.

He handed what he called a "preliminary paper" to an officer of the Physico-Medical Society of Würzburg on December 28, 1895. The report was printed at once by the *Stahelsche K. Hof- und Universitäts Buch und Kunsthandlung* and distributed during the first days of January 1896.

In his preliminary report he told the world how he established the existence of these new rays called X rays. He told about the penetrating qualities of the rays and also told about the shadow of the hand and how the bones produced a strange image on the plate.

At about the same time he sent the first X-ray pictures to his friend, Professor E. Warburg, Director of the Warburg Physical Institute in Berlin. The X rays were one of many exhibits used at the celebration of the fiftieth anniversary of the institute on January 4, 1896.

The program of the meeting said, "On exhibition are a

series of photographs, which Herr Roentgen made with the X rays recently discovered by him."

The people at the meeting didn't seem excited or interested. His photographs seemed to be just another announcement of another new piece of research.

A scientist, R. Neuhass, saw the pictures at the Warburg Institute and described them:

A compass in a metal box had produced on the plate a black picture of the magnetic needle. Another picture showed various steps of a shadow scale which had been formed by a ladder of tinfoil. A set of weights enclosed in a wooden box and a covered wire spiral wrapped on a heavy wooden block showed distinct pictures of the metal but only weak shadows of the wood. But the most curious picture is that of a human hand.

At the banquet in the Hotel Reichshof that night, the President of the Physical Society, W. von Bezold, talked about all the instructive demonstrations in the Physical Institute. But he never mentioned Roentgen's discovery.

The pictures had been put over in a corner of the exhibition hall. Although they were right there for all to see, most didn't notice them. The most learned scientists and professors in Germany walked right by the first X-ray pictures.

16

Center of the Storm

Almost as soon as Roentgen discovered the rays, he sent nine photographs along with his news to Austria, where his friend Franz Exner was a professor at the University of Vienna. He and Franz had studied and worked together in Zurich and in Strasbourg.

Although he could not know it, his packet arrived on the same day Exner usually met with other scientists to talk about what was new in science. Professor Exner showed the group the pictures he just received from Würzburg. Ernest Lecer, a scientist from Prague, was at the meeting that evening and asked if he could borrow the pictures for a short time.

About midnight, still on that same evening, he showed the pictures to his father, Z. K. Lecer, who was the editor of a newspaper, the *Presse*. What was not obvious to the scientists at the meeting of the fiftieth anniversary of the Warburg Institute was clearly obvious to the newspaper editor.

He immediately knew that this was a world-shaking piece of news. Could his son give him some facts to go with the pictures? Then the *Presse* printed what the older Lecer wrote. At the end of the article he pleaded, "The *Presse* assures its readers that there is no joke or humbug in the matter. It is a serious discovery by a serious German professor."

That newspaper article in Vienna was the spark that sent news of X rays exploding all over the globe. It was one of the very few times the entire world could agree on anything. In the next few days and weeks most of mankind joined together to celebrate Roentgen's fantastic scientific discovery.

Everyone was curious about something. And the world believed that Wilhelm Roentgen had given it a way to satisfy its curiosity about everything. X rays could be the tool used to find out what was inside: with X-ray photographs everyone could learn about everything.

Almost as soon as it appeared in the *Vienna Presse*, the *London Standard* printed the news on January 7. Then even a far-off American paper, the *Electrical Engineer* in New York City, printed it on January 8. Newspapers in Russia, France and even Japan quickly carried the story of X rays.

The newspapers in Würzburg, closest to Roentgen, were among the last to write about the rays. After traveling halfway around the world, the news of his discovery was finally reported in his own city. On January 9, twelve days after he handed the preliminary report to the President of the Würzburg Physico-Medical Society, the *Würzburger Generalanzeiger* finally announced the news, and misspelled his name.

All of this was unexpected. Most surprising of all to Roentgen was the public's reaction to the idea of X rays. Certainly most readers were not thinking of X rays as a scientific tool or as an interesting problem in physics. Depending on who wrote about X rays, Roentgen had uncovered a new toy, a new weapon, a new instrument, a new subject for poets and reporters, a new reason for new laws, and only last a new territory for scientific research.

It was most astonishing to him and to Bertha. But it began to happen.

Slowly at first, almost as one raindrop then another and another and another falls, with more and more pelting down faster and faster and faster, so the invitations and visitors from the world began to shower down on him and Bertha.

Neither of them could understand it. Certainly they never expected it. The well-wishers, the reporters, the curious, all began to crowd into his laboratory. He and his family, it seemed, were the center of a gigantic stage. The whole world was watching them, sending them letters, calling on them, asking them to parties, asking him to give demonstrations and lectures.

He was being treated like some sort of hero. And Bertha was being treated as the hero's wife. Soon it was not only scientists, but emperors and even presidents from foreign countries that were trying to reach him.

He didn't want any part of the party. Just as the world could congratulate you one day, it could just as easily tell you that you were not good enough on the next. It wasn't that many years back that Würzburg, the very university that was now honoring him, had told him that he was not good enough to teach there.

Complaining to a friend, he wrote:

On January first I sent out the first offprints and then all hell broke loose! The *Presse* in Vienna was the first to blast the trumpet to the world and the others followed. After a few weeks I was disgusted with the whole thing. I could not even recognize my own work on reading the reports. Photography was only a means to me and yet this was made the main discovery. Slowly I got used to all the racket, but the storm cost time; I could not do a single experiment for four full weeks. Other people could work — but I could not. You have no idea what went on.

One of the scientists who didn't like the whole idea of invisible rays was A. E. Dobear of Tufts College, who wrote in the *Electrical World*:

It must seem like a ghostly experiment to photograph the skeleton of a living person as though it was dissected out and articulated with wires. But the same process has its threatening aspect. If one can photograph through wood, blank walls, and in the dark too, then privacy is impossible; for it will be light everywhere but to one's eyes, and for these there will be substitutes.

It was no wonder that some people were frightened. According to the poems, songs, cartoons and magazine articles, X rays could somehow penetrate in a way no one had ever dreamed possible. If you wore eyeglasses with X-ray lenses, could X rays help you see through the clothes someone was wearing? Some shops already advertised "X-ray proof" underclothing — made of lead.

Many protested the printing of his "ghost pictures." One of the magazines, *The Electrician*, January 10, 1896, claimed, "We cannot, however, agree with the newspapers in regarding this discovery as a revolution in photography; there are few persons who would care to sit for a portrait which would show only the bones and rings on the fingers."

In far-off America, a lawmaker, Assemblyman Reed of Somerset County in New Jersey, introduced a bill into the House of Representatives at Trenton, New Jersey, on February 19, 1896, prohibiting the use of X rays in opera glasses in theaters.

Yet, in spite of some panic, there didn't seem to be one corner of the world that didn't want to know more about X rays. And Roentgen was the only one who knew anything at all about them. The whole world, it seemed to him, suddenly turned to him and his laboratory for all the answers to their questions.

17

Convincing the World

Until that announcement in early January of 1896 few Germans had heard of Wilhelm Roentgen or thought much of Würzburg except as a religious center. They knew that, like the waters of the river flowing through Würzburg, like the travelers hurrying through Würzburg to get to another part of Germany, true excitement in the shape of exceptional happenings had never stopped there.

The people of Würzburg, at the university and in the town itself, were satisfied that this should be so. They seemed quite content to live their ordinary lives — to work, to farm, to hunt, to attend their church meetings, to go to choir practice, and to their club meetings and on their holidays.

When Roentgen first noticed those crystals glowing in the blackness of his laboratory, not a soul sleeping in Würzburg, certainly not even he, dreamed that almost overnight he would change all that peace. That within two weeks Würzburg would become a world center. Afterward, for years to come, the townsfolk and the people at the university would know that they were alive at a time when and living in a place where one of their own neighbors had made a discovery that changed the world.

Roentgen had never wanted to become famous. All he had ever wanted was to be known by a few, those scientists and professors he respected the most. He didn't care about the rest. But this was not to be his fate. Peace was gone for him and for Bertha, it seemed, forever.

Even the Emperor of Germany was curious about X rays. Wilhelm II, grandson of England's Queen Victoria, had become Emperor of Germany in 1888. He believed that everything from Germany was first-rate. It had the best of everything, including the best army. Now Germany was superior in science, too. To the Kaiser the discovery of X rays meant that Germany was as victorious in science as it was on the battlefield.

Like the rest of the world, the Kaiser wanted to know more about X rays. And so he invited, really commanded, Roentgen to give a demonstration of X rays before members of the royal family and the German court, on January 13, 1896, in Potsdam.

The next day, the newspaper *Nieus Wiener Tageblatt* reported the demonstration:

Last night at five o'clock Professor Roentgen demonstrated his discovery before the Kaiser and Kaiserin, Kaiserin Friedrich, Boase, Lucanus, and other distinguished persons. Roentgen could not give a demonstration on a large scale because the necessary instruments were not readily obtainable. However, he showed several experiments in which the new rays penetrated wooden boards and cardboard boxes, and he also photographed a few lifeless objects but not the human hand. After dinner the Kaiser remained with Roentgen and the other guests until midnight. The Kaiser personally decorated Roentgen with the "Kronenorden, Second Class."

Later, Roentgen learned, there was a rumor that the Emperor had wanted to see if X rays could photograph his withered left arm, perhaps even to help cure it.

But Roentgen would not comment on the rumor, or talk about all the other royalty and rich people who asked for help and healing with X rays.

Day after day the invitations, requests and commands from the highest in science and in politics came, asking him to talk about X rays. Finally, he closed the door of his laboratory on the commotion. All the world could talk about X rays but he had no time to waste.

If he were to continue as the true discoverer of X rays he had to stay ahead of all the other scientists who were now working on them. There had to be a second communication after his first. There was still a great deal to learn about X rays.

Just as important, he had plans for many other new investigations. He did not intend his life to center round or to end with discovery of X rays. He couldn't wait to close out his work on the X rays. Then he would move on to other fields in physics.

But it was expected of him, he knew, that he give a

lecture before the members of the society whose magazine printed his preliminary report. And so, on January 23, 1896, he appeared before the Physico-Medical Society of Würzburg.

They told him the crowd had started coming hours before his lecture. When it was time for him to begin, the room was packed. As he glanced around that night, he knew that there were many more there than just the members of the society. Besides members of the Physico-Medical Society were professors, other scientists, high city officials, representatives of the army, royalty, and of course, many students, all jammed together to hear what he had to say.

It was reassuring, at least, to hear the storm of applause that greeted him as he entered that night. It was as if the audience had already heard what he was going to say and had already accepted all of it as a scientific truth. But even while he was talking, he knew in his heart that there was much more work to do on X rays.

Because of the general interest, he told them, he thought it his duty to speak publicly about his *Arbeit* — his work — although the experiments were still in development. Before he described his own work, he first gave credit for investigations on cathode rays by other scientists: Heinrich Hertz, Philipp Lenard, and others who led him to make experiments along the same lines.

Then he described the moment he first saw the fluorescence of a small piece of paper coated with barium platinocyanide. He told how the shimmering light appeared every time he sent an electrical charge through the tube covered with the light-tight cardboard. How the tube itself and not any other part of the apparatus was responsible for the strange happening. Finally: "I found by accident that the rays penetrated black paper. I then used wood, paper, books, but I still believed I was the victim of deception. Finally I used photography and the experiment was successfully culminated."

Explaining that there was much more work to be done, he showed them the X-ray pictures of weights in a box, a compass, the wire wound on a piece of wood, and last, a picture of a human hand. And the lecture was over.

In all the dreams he had ever dared to dream as a schoolboy, he had never imagined that he would be the center of all this goodwill, this applause, this excitement. At last the world recognized in him what he and few others had also seen — that he had something different, something unusual, something exciting to give to it. And they were accepting his gift and they were thanking him for it.

In the midst of the hubbub, while they were still congratulating him, His Excellency, Rudolf von Kölliker, the famous professor of anatomy at Würzburg, came up to him. Would His Excellency permit them to photograph his hand? The famous anatomy professor quickly agreed, and Roentgen took the picture. While the crowd waited, he developed it and showed it to them.

Turning to the crowd after all the hand-clapping subsided, the older man told it: "During the forty-eight years I have been a member of the Physico-Medical Society, I never have attended a meeting at which a subject of such great significance has been presented. In my opinion, the discovery will be of utmost significance in the natural sciences and perhaps also in medicine. . . ." He led the audience in three cheers for Roentgen. If that was not enough, he proposed that henceforth the rays be called "Roentgen rays."

Then von Kölliker asked Roentgen: "In time, would it be possible to make X-ray photographs of the human body? Could surgery and anatomy benefit by the discovery?" According to the demonstrations, he continued, it did not seem possible "at this time because the different organs, nerves, muscles and veins were all of approximately the same density, and so it would be difficult to tell the difference between them by the rays, which only produced a definite shadow for bones."

Then another surgeon, Professor C. Schönborn, warned them all against "too much optimism, since X rays promise to be scarcely of any value in the diagnosis of internal disturbances." Answering quickly, Roentgen assured Professor Schönborn that "it is not difficult to photograph a dog or cat according to my method, and it will be possible in the near future to make X-ray pictures of larger parts of the human body. I am not a doctor or a surgeon," he told the group, "and I do not have time to continue my experiments in that direction. But I would be willing to lend the help of my experience for any such experiments made in medical institutions."

The others didn't realize it, but Roentgen did. That lecture on January 23, 1896, was going to be the only one he would ever give before a large audience on X rays.

18

Price of Fame

A week passed, and then another, and another. Snow covered the cobblestone streets, and the mountains around them stood silently capped in ice white. It appeared to be a peaceful time of year, when little could be done outside and everyone stayed indoors. But that peace was not to be found in Roentgen's laboratory.

Offers of titles were pouring in from Germany and from foreign countries as well. The Kingdom of Bavaria offered him the Royal Merit of the Crown. It meant that he could use the word "von" before his last name. As "von Roentgen" he would be a nobleman. But he didn't want it. He accepted the decoration but refused the title.

Offers of honorary membership and awards arrived daily from foreign scientific societies. It was easiest to say "no" to all of them rather than to waste time deciding which one to accept and which one to refuse. Some were equally important or equally unimportant.

One of the few he did accept came from his birthplace, the city of Lennep, Germany. The city council made him a citizen on April 18, 1896. Even though he was born in Germany, he really didn't think of it as home. He had always thought of Holland as his home because he grew up there.

It was a race now for the honor of announcing even more new information about X rays. As always, credit for an announcement depended on the date of the publication of the news and not on the date of the discovery. Many other scientists were now rushing to start research on X rays to get their names into print and claim credit.

As soon as they had heard about X rays, these other researchers had rushed back to their laboratories to check Roentgen's thinking. He knew his experiments were being repeated in physical and medical laboratories of universities, in high schools, in photography studios and even by some curious individuals.

Chemists, physicists, electrical engineers, doctors, surgeons, photographers, all started experimenting with X rays. Almost at once, doctors were competing with doctors, engineers with engineers. News traveled from one country to another, all compared notes, photographs, and ideas. "X rays" as a topic was listed on the programs of all the important scientific meetings. New clubs and societies began springing up all over the world — all formed only to find out more about X rays.

The demands on the manufacturers of electrical equipment for X-ray research was so great that they could not fill the orders. Instrument-makers and glass-blowers were swamped with orders for tubes and screens.

Roentgen knew all too well that with all the research

going on around him he had to publish that second paper on X rays quickly. If he didn't, some other scientist could claim part of his discovery.

Slamming the door of his laboratory, he refused to see anyone. He refused to give talks and answer questions from other laboratories, and he declined honors. He stopped trying to explain why he would not see reporters, nor even the very important visitors, nor the curiosity seekers who seemed to be swarming over his institute every day. He gave out only one interview to a magazine. That was when a reporter came all the way from America just to talk to him about his discovery. He allowed the reporter to come and visit, and H. S. W. Damm wrote an article, "The New Marvel in Photography," for the April 1896 issue of *McClure's* magazine.

Roentgen kept his old schedule. Even while he was finding out more about X rays, he still designed and built his own new equipment, went over older experiments, and then began his new research.

If all of this was difficult for him, he could see it was doubly so for Bertha. He could lock the door to his laboratory and insist that no one bother him but Bertha was far too polite to do that.

Although she did not say too much to him, she did complain to her cousin, Louise Roentgen-Grauel, who lived far away in the United States, in Indiana. Bertha wrote on March 4, 1896:

Wilhelm has so much work he doesn't know which way to turn. Yes, dear Louise, it is not a small matter to become a

101

famous man, and few people realize how much work and unrest this carries with it. When Wilhelm told me in November that he was working on an interesting problem, we had no idea how it would be received, but as soon as the paper was published our domestic peace was gone.

Every day I am astonished at the enormous working capacity of my husband, and that he can keep his thoughts on his work in spite of the thousand little things with which he is annoyed. But now it is high time that he should rest, and I am preparing everything for our departure, because we are going down south for a few weeks, in order to permit Wilhelm to spend all his time in the open. Every day I am grateful to God that He made him so healthy and strong, and yet often I am fearful that someday the strain may become too much for him.

But now I talk only of the less lovely part of our experiences and have not said a word about our great happiness over the success of his work. Our hearts are full of gratitude that we are permitted to live through such a wonderful experience. How many recognitions has my dear received for his indefatigable research! Often we are almost dizzy with all the praise and honors. It would be alarming if the man who received all this were vain. But you know my honest, modest husband as scarcely anyone else does, and you can understand that he finds his highest reward in the fact that he was permitted to accomplish something valuable in serving pure science.

Struggling for time, Roentgen paused for just a little while to consider what was happening. And, from where he was, he could see that people all over the world had acted much the same way when they heard about X rays.

At first, people were astonished, even shocked. At the

next step they repeated the experiments he had done and agreed that he was indeed correct, that he had covered all there was to say about X rays, that there was little more reason for more research except to carry it one step further and make more accurate measurements. Then the last stage was to realize that there was room for more research, because there were many areas Roentgen had not covered.

This last stage was the most reassuring to Roentgen because it meant that there would be competition among the scientists — fiercer than that of any sporting event.

He knew that researchers were working day and night to be the first with new facts about X rays.

Suddenly there was so much new information about X rays that the newspapers and scientific journals could not keep up with the announcements. The British scientific journal *Nature* objected to what was happening and printed the following complaint:

> So numerous are the communications being made to scientific societies that it is difficult to keep pace with them, and the limits of our space would be exceeded if we attempted to describe the whole of the contributions to the subjects, even at this early stage.

Those other researchers weren't the only ones to be experimenting with X rays. Roentgen himself had been working day and night for weeks. Just ten weeks after his first paper, on March 9, 1896, he finished his second communication.

103

The officers of the Physico-Medical Society eagerly accepted it for publication and printed it in their journal. Soon it was printed as a separate pamphlet.

This time, Roentgen reported that he had invented a scale for measuring the intensity of the rays. He found that if exposed to X rays, electrified bodies in air would discharge the electrical charge they were carrying, and that if the air was replaced by hydrogen, the rate of the electrical discharge was reduced.

He also reported that any solid body could be made to generate X rays when cathode rays were directed upon it. In addition, he said he knew no reason why liquids or gases could not be made to behave in the same manner.

By now, he knew there were two different ideas among the scientists about X rays. One group insisted that they were of the same nature as ordinary light. Some from this group argued among themselves as to what kind of light. Then the other group believed that X rays were cathode rays. But as for him, he really didn't belong to either group. To him, X rays were X rays, and nothing more. He simply went on studying X rays as X rays.

There was also a good deal of guessing as to who first found X rays and when that was. Sure, it was true that Roentgen was the first to realize what they were, but no one thought for a moment that he really was the very first one to produce X rays.

Somewhere in the world at some time back in history, X rays had been produced by other scientists. Perhaps it was hundreds of years earlier. They might have been produced as early as 1700 by Francis Hauksbee, a scientist who died in 1713. Almost two hundred years before Roentgen, Hauksbee had been experimenting with a vacuum when he observed glow discharges and many other new and curious happenings. Another scientist, Abbe Jean Nollet, who died in 1770, experimented with the "electrical egg" and made fundamental observations which may have included X rays. None of these people or the ones who followed identified what they were seeing.

Wilhelm Conrad Roentgen was the first to understand just what he was looking at. He was the first to understand that what he was looking at was something new, different and totally unexplainable.

His discovery represented the sudden bringing together of much of the scientific research and development of the past three hundred years. Some of these developments were: the production of the vacuum, increased understanding of the natures of electricity, magnetism, and light, understanding of what matter and crystals were made of, and the study of electric discharges in a vacuum.

Perhaps that was why, at the time of Roentgen's discovery, the science of physics was considered complete except for the addition of more decimal points to measurements. What he and the others could not realize was that his discovery marked the beginning of a complete change in science and a revolution in physics. For, from the study of X rays, there would come the discovery of radioactivity, which would change the course of the world forever.

It would take scientists another ten years to come up

with the answers to what X rays really were. Much as Roentgen wanted to explain what they were, and how they worked, neither he nor the other scientists could do it at the time. For now, all he could say was that X rays were a form of energy, just as light is a form of energy. . . . That the human eye could only see a limited range of light, so it could not see X rays.

Ten years later, scientists would find that, somehow, the electrons dashing through the tube were connected to X rays. They would also learn that when the electrons were shot against a solid block of metal and brought to a sudden stop against the metal, then it gave off X rays.

In the tube he used, Roentgen had slammed the electrons against the metal block with a tremendous force. As they smacked into the solid block of metal, the electrons produced the penetrating X rays.

Without the electron tube, there wouldn't have been any X rays. Without X rays there wouldn't have been any experiments trying to find out what the X rays were. And from these studies about X rays, there would one day be still more findings which would sound to the people of Roentgen's time like stories of the unreal and supernatural.

19

Problems, Rumors, and Rewards

It was far easier for all the countries of the world to accept the idea of these invisible X rays than it was for them to agree on a name for them. Only the Germans, it seemed, were happy with the name "Roentgen rays."

Finally, in America, a questionnaire was sent out on March 20, 1896, by the magazine *Electrical World*. It went to all well-known American scientists who were working with the rays. It asked them to make suggestions for the proper name. At the same time, the same questionnaire was also sent out in England by the *British Medical Journal*. The names sent back were: skiagraphy, skotography, skigraphy, shadow print, roentography, roentgenograph, roentgen picture, radiography, radio photography, electro-skiography, ixography, cathodography, diagraphy, actinography, pykoscopy, and dark light.

Of course it wasn't possible to agree and select just one. It was easier to let the name drift. The English-speaking countries used the name radiography and X-ray photography; the German countries called it Roentgen photography.

Now that all the world needed, wanted, and used the X ray, who was going to own it? Most people expected that Roentgen would take out a patent on the X ray. A patent meant that the government would give him a grant, as the inventor, for a stated period of time, a monopoly of the exclusive right to make, use, and sell his discovery. With the whole world clamoring for X rays, this could certainly make him and Bertha very rich.

But he did not intend to become rich through the X rays. According to the tradition of all good German university professors, Roentgen wanted his discoveries and inventions to belong to mankind. They should not in any way be hampered by patents, licenses, or contracts, nor be controlled by one group.

The Americans were the first to attempt to buy his discovery, "holding millions before my eyes," but he insisted "no patents be taken out." In this way he was making it possible for ever greater numbers of scientists to work with Roentgen rays.

He didn't think much of getting copyrights to his first pictures. By now millions of copies were being sold all over the world. The editor of the *British Journal of Photography* stated: "If the now famous Roentgen ray skiagraphs had been made copyright, a very large sum could have been obtained for permission to use them as soon as the rays were 'boomed' and what a boom there was and has been."

Even the tube makers, the talented ones who made the instruments used for Roentgen's experiments, refused to take out patents. The well-known glass-blower, Goetze, in Leipzig, took the same stand as Roentgen did and was absolutely opposed to copyrighting any part of the experiment or equipment.

That first year after the discovery, it seemed as if the world, scientists as well as businessmen, didn't want to make a profit on the X rays. For one of the few times in history all mankind agreed on something: X rays should be used for the good of the world.

Or almost all mankind. There were a few, it seemed, who realized that the X rays could make large amounts of money. And so they were busy finding new ways to use them for profit.

One of the busiest was a United States inventor in New Jersey by the name of Thomas Alva Edison. He was best known for inventing electrical devices. He had heard about the rays and begun experiments on X-ray detection two days after the news reached America.

In four days, Roentgen learned, Edison had repeated the basic experiments and gave the facts to twenty newspapermen who were invited to his laboratories to get the news about the new rays. Twelve of the twenty remained at his laboratories for two weeks. He was known to be careful about everything he published. Before he had finished, Edison had his assistant examine the fluorescent properties of eighteen hundred substances before he chose calcium tungstate as the most suitable material.

Then he created still another invention and named it the fluoroscope.

"The fluoroscope was a tube or box, fitted with a screen coated with a fluorescent substance, used for viewing objects exposed to X rays. It was going to be the beginning of one of the most important ways of using X rays, to help in the treatment of the sick."

Edison arranged a special exhibition on Roentgen rays at the electrical exhibit in New York in May 1896.

After a vacation in Italy in March, the Roentgens found that there was even more excitement about the X rays. The noise about them had not died down.

Invitations to all the parties, all the speeches, all the meetings to honor him were still pouring in, all the magazine articles written about his invention were still coming out, all the people from all the organizations all trying to persuade, beg or invite him and sometimes even Bertha, too, were still swarming over him.

However, Roentgen still would not become part of the circus that now seemed to have claimed his X rays.

Even though others were now making speeches explaining the X rays, and some were now claiming all kinds of new inventions having to do with X rays, the world would not leave him alone. In May he was elected a corresponding member of the Berlin Academy of Sciences, in November, of the Munich Academy of Sciences.

The foreign countries were just as insistent. Invitations to come to their meetings, or to become a member of their scientific societies, poured in from all over the world.

The British Association for the Advancement of Science invited him to their meetings — he refused. The Royal Society in London, at its annual meeting in November 1896, awarded him the golden Rumford medal. The Italian government appointed him Komtur of the Order of the Italian Crown.

In March 1897, Roentgen published his third communication on the X rays: "Further Observations on the Properties of X rays." This time he sent it to the Prussian Academy of Sciences in Berlin rather than to the Physico-Medical Society of Würzburg, where he had sent the first two. It would be the last paper on X rays he would publish for many years.

In this paper he told how he had worked only on the intensity of radiation and how to measure it. He showed that the tubes used in X rays were important.

Using the same power supply and apparatus but changing the tubes, he was able to get a ray five times as powerful. He named the more penetrating rays "hard" rays, and those that were weaker "soft" rays. He showed how to use "hard" or "soft" rays depending on what was going to be photographed. If, for instance, the bone structure of a hand was to be photographed, a hard ray was used, but for the fleshy parts, a soft ray was used.

Then, before he ended his final report, he told what other facts needed to be found out about X rays. He wanted to search out only what the rays were made of and how they acted, rather than how they could be used, or how they could be produced better.

111

20

The Nobel Prize

The next few years were all a busy blur of honors, students, research, and of course vacations and friends.

By December 1899, four years after Roentgen discovered X rays, he was asked to accept the Chair of Experimental Physics and become director of the Institute of Physics of the University of Munich. This time he could not refuse the special request of the Bavarian government. It meant he and Bertha would have to move halfway across Germany to the Bavarian capital of Munich.

The Roentgens weren't concerned about the move; what did concern them was the kind of people they found there. And they didn't like what they found. Bertha and he had been happier at Würzburg than at any other place they ever lived — except possibly Giessen. Even their fame was easier to live with in Würzburg. Their closest friends in Würzburg had not treated them as if they were royalty or set apart from the rest. When they moved from Würzburg, they forever left the last place they were treated as an ordinary professor and his wife.

Neither of them wanted to move away. But they had to. And that was that.

Almost as soon as they moved to Munich, they were sorry. They had many reasons for not wanting to come, but what happened was totally unexpected. Somehow a rumor got started that Roentgen was not cooperative. It was difficult to get along with him.

When they got to the root of the rumor, they found it had begun when he rejected the offer to use the word "von" before his name to make him a nobleman. His refusal was well known in court circles. The people of the court were still slightly angry with him. When he refused the title, he had made it appear unimportant.

The senseless rumor even affected the man with the highest education post in all of Germany. The Bavarian minister of education was also convinced that Roentgen was not easy to get along with.

It didn't take Roentgen long to begin a war of his own with that minister of education. He needed money for his laboratory equipment, and somehow he had to get the money from that minister.

He later wrote to his friend Theodor Boveri about the minister of education in Munich:

So many things could be beautiful and good in Munich if there were not some people who are chiefly convinced of their own importance without, however, sufficient reason. In addition to this, the minister of education is a bureaucrat and has no real interest in the development and the progress of the university, probably because he is not familiar with conditions. It is really a miracle and a sign of great inner strength that science in Germany makes so much progress in spite of ministers and other impediments.

At the same time he was struggling with the ministry of education for money to reorganize his department, he was still being showered with honors from foreign countries. Columbia University in New York City awarded him a medal in 1900 at the suggestion of the Academy of Sciences. The medal, given every five years, was called the Barnard Medal.

Naturally, Roentgen did not go to America for the ceremony for the medal. He had much too much to do at Munich.

Then he heard that the Roentgen Society of the United States of America had been founded in St. Louis, Missouri; it was the first medical society devoted to X rays.

Where would all of this end?

In spite of all the honors and duties that took up so much of his time, he was supposed to do as much work as anyone else. In the eyes of the system, he was just another teacher, and nothing more.

But if the educators didn't seem to like him, at least his students did. And that was what really mattered.

His lecture room — one of the largest — was always jammed. He couldn't believe that so many students were interested in physics. A little later, he began to understand that some didn't care about experimental physics. They only came in order to see him and to say afterward, "I was there."

But in spite of being a popular lecturer and having

many students who knew little about science sit in on his classes, Roentgen would not make a game out of his work, nor would he use anything but scientific language. There were many chemists, physicists, and young medical students who needed the information he was teaching. If anyone else couldn't understand him, he could leave.

He didn't think much of popular lectures on X rays or on physics. He told his students:

Physics is a science which must be proved with honest effort. One can, perchance, present a subject in such a manner that an audience of laymen may be convinced erroneously that it has understood the lecture. This, however, means furthering a superficial knowledge which is worse and more dangerous than none at all.

He never repeated the same lecture year after year, as he knew other professors were doing. He made sure that his experiments showed the young students how to work. Whenever he could, he would add a new discovery to the lecture demonstration. Even so, he knew that the medical students, particularly, could not or did not like his lectures. Some thought them dry or boring, or were disappointed and stayed away from them. But he didn't care. He knew lectures were designed for those who were trying to follow what he said and who had an understanding of the basics in physics.

By now, Roentgen had almost everything he wanted. He knew that as one of the "greats" in science he and Bertha could go anywhere or do anything they wanted to.

Yet he still found himself nervous and easily frightened by strangers, who were, it seemed, interested in him only because he was famous. In spite of knowing what he wanted from the world and getting it, he still found that it was difficult for him and Bertha to make new friends in Munich.

Of course, there were all the official parties and meetings to go to — even the Munich Oktoberfest, a beer feast and an annual event in Munich since 1810. But he and Bertha missed the Boveris and the other friends they left behind at Würzburg.

There were more and more stories that others had discovered the X rays and not he. One attack after the other repeated the story that he was not the first to notice X rays, that he had nothing to do with the medical application of X rays, that that first X-ray picture of a hand was made as a suggestion from another scientist present in the laboratory. And then there were the complaints from another scientist, Philipp Lenard, who had also investigated cathode rays and who said that his early experiments were the basis for Roentgen's own discovery. Sometimes Roentgen felt: "It is almost as if I have to apologize for discovering the rays."

He also saw that Bertha was not feeling well, although she did not complain too much. He knew it was difficult for her to put up with guests when she was in pain. So, not only he, but Bertha too, tried to keep away from all the strangers they were meeting.

For them to be treated as everyone else was difficult.

He learned he now was being nominated for a prize of money, the first one of its kind ever given. A movement had been formed to do away with all wars, and several rich industrialists gave large contributions to funds to help promote peace. One of them, Alfred Nobel, a Swedish chemist, had willed the major part of a huge fortune he made from the manufacture of dynamite and other high explosives to a fund of this kind. He set up prizes for people who helped the cause of international peace as well as prizes for those who advanced the cause of science and literature. The Nobel Peace Prize began in 1901, and together with four other awards for work in physiology, or medicine, physics, chemistry and literature, was his idea.

Even with this great honor, Roentgen had to live by the rules. And so he wrote to the Bavarian Ministry of State in Munich on December 6, 1901, asking for a leave of absence in order to go to Stockholm to receive the Nobel Prize. It was granted.

And so he took a holiday from Munich to travel to Stockholm to receive the Nobel Prize for physics in person. Bertha didn't go, though. It seemed better, with her poor health, for her to remain behind at home rather than to fight the deep cold of the Swedish winter with its long dark days.

21

Bertha

When Roentgen was finally settled at the hotel in Stockholm, December 9, 1901, he wrote to Bertha:

I just received your telegram and read it with pleasure. The letter arrived by the same train as I, but I think that it probably was not so seasick.

It was a bad day yesterday. We had rain with strong southern winds from the time we left Berlin. The boat in Sassnitz is good, but not very large and was thrown up and down like a nutshell. The waves constantly broke over the boat so that it was impossible to be in the open air. . . . The formal celebration is tomorrow evening at seven o'clock, followed by a supper, and for the next day there are many invitations from professors. I shall probably decline them and return soon. . . . Sweden is covered with snow, and though the sun isn't shining, it isn't raining or snowing. . . . Stockholm is a very peculiar city. More the next time.

Roentgen knew he would be expected to give a lecture before all the other prizewinners, the committee, even the nobility of Sweden, after he was officially presented with

118

the medal and the prize money. But he refused, preferring instead to express his thanks the next evening, at the formal banquet in the mosaic-decorated Golden Room of Stockholm's town hall.

Just as Nobel wanted to work for peace, Roentgen also wanted to help the public. He announced to the assembly that he would contribute his talent and energy, and even the Nobel Prize money of fifty thousand Swedish kronor [about thirteen thousand dollars] to increase the potential of science to help people. A professor should do what he could to help the public good. To show them that he really meant it, he donated the prize money to the University of Würzburg.

The Nobel Prize did not help the Roentgens make any friends in Munich. In fact, it set them even further apart from the other professors. The only friends he and Bertha continued to be really at ease with were those from the earlier days at Giessen and Würzburg.

It had been four years since his last paper on X rays, written in 1897. In those last four years he knew all too well that others were getting rich on his discovery. But he would not have anything to do with making money from X rays. Let others make fortunes — as for him, all he wanted now was to have people leave him and Bertha alone. Year after year it seemed, as he grew older, he was becoming more and more famous the world over. The only place where he and Bertha could hide was in the mountain village of Weilheim, where they owned a cottage. He would not think of inviting the other professors from the faculty to Weilheim, but his students knew they were always welcome.

Whenever he could, he would climb the steepest mountains on hiking trips.

They had the hunting lodge rebuilt into a very pleasant summer home, which contrasted with the dark and stiff furniture in their formal apartment back in Munich. He and Bertha hung pictures of small animals and hunting scenes; he also insisted that they hang some trophies of his hunts — antlers and stuffed birds.

Even his clothes were different from the ones in Munich. While in the big city he always wore his big round city hat, which he always tried to protect carefully from every drop of rain. But out in the country, he jammed his old and shabby feathered hat on his head and outfitted himself with a greenish-gray hunting suit.

The years seemed to pass more quickly now that he and Bertha were getting older. Even though it was suddenly 1913, a dozen years since winning the Nobel Prize, he and Bertha were still being treated as if they were famous. And they still did not like it.

His brain was still expertly racing along with the newest advances in science. Yet his body seemed to be telling him it was time to let up. Especially after faculty meetings, it seemed, he would suddenly feel dizzy — a vertigo that made everything in the room whirl around him. Any sort of hard work would bring the dizziness on. Then he had two hemorrhages from his lungs.

As if this was not enough, in February of 1913, Roentgen

noticed a rather solid swelling behind his left ear, the one that had become deaf.

Bertha and the Boveris kept trying to convince him that he should have it operated on. He didn't want an operation; he didn't want to worry Bertha and he wondered if he would survive it. Yet at last there seemed to be no choice.

The operation over, he began to feel better after that summer of 1913. This time his body did not try to hold back his mind. Work had not seemed as easy in years. But now it was Bertha who felt more and more weak all the time. Over the years, Bertha's illness and attacks of colic in her kidneys had gotten worse and worse. She was suffering more and more from those convulsions in her kidneys.

Once Roentgen wrote to Theodor Boveri:

It is my impression that my poor wife is continually growing worse; and this, in spite of the fact that there are occasional signs of improvement which are, however, becoming rarer and rarer. Narcotics must be used almost daily. But, with very few exceptions, she is always very brave.

He wouldn't leave the house now. To help her stand the suffering, Bertha was receiving five injections of pain-killing morphine a day. Roentgen wouldn't let anyone else give them to her.

By December of 1914 he wrote again to Boveri from Munich:

In regard to the morphine syringe . . . you are right when you say that one has to use it according to one's own judgment . . . at one time the family physician says, "Do not spare any morphine," and on another occasion . . . "Increase the dose only very slowly." Nobody could tell me at what time of the day the injections should be given or how the doses should be distributed. We have had to find it out for ourselves.

It seemed that the world suddenly closed in on them, centering on the house, on Bertha, on her pain. Their lives now were being planned around the "what ifs." If they traveled, what if Bertha had a severe attack? What if he could not get experienced doctors? What if he could not manage to get her home?

The world outside was in trouble. But let politics and politicians worry about nations. He had to worry about Bertha. Yet he found he couldn't really ignore the world.

On August 3, 1914, Germany declared war on France. Somewhere he knew dimly that there was trouble — but certainly not a war! Yes, there was now a war. A total world war. It involved every great power of Europe, together with Japan and the United States and most lesser powers of the world. Nothing mankind had ever known before equaled it in its destructiveness or its ugliness.

It was a terrific shock to him, to Europe. In an instant, dreams of peaceful progress had blown away. Yet, right from the start, he, like the others, expected that the war would be a short one, and Germany would win. Certainly at the beginning the strategy of the German military seemed to be working. Their plan was to strike first with stronger armies in the west against France, and then when France was crushed to turn eastward and overwhelm Russia.

Huge German armies overcame all resistance in Belgium and drove France's army and Britain's "expeditionary force" backward toward Paris.

Roentgen, like all the others, was doing everything he could to help the German cause. Yet, he could not say that he hated the enemy — the French and the English — even though he gave up the English Rumford Medal of gold to be melted down for bullion. In later years he would regret this.

Almost in spite of the war, it seemed, people remembered him and his birthday. There was even a letter from Paul von Hindenburg, the leader of the German army, telling him how useful his Roentgen rays were in helping the wounded.

At the beginning, all the fighting nations, even Germany, thought it would be another short war. But all at once, they realized that the struggle would be long and costly. The First World War lasted four years and fifteen weeks. It was waged by thirty nations, including all the great powers. Sixty-five million men fought in it. Eight and a half million were killed, twenty-nine million were wounded, captured or missing. The direct costs of the war were estimated as something like two hundred billion dollars. What it cost in property and in lives would never be counted.

The downfall of the imperial German government and the succession of a republican and socialist government caught Roentgen by surprise — almost as much of a surprise as had the sudden collapse of the German army.

In August 1914, it seemed that Germany could easily

walk right through Europe. But in September, almost in sight of Paris, the Germans were halted by the French and British, and in the next three days, in a series of actions known as the Battle of the Marne, they were forced to retreat. By September 14, the Germans were on the defensive.

Now victory would not come so fast for the Germans. The war seemed at a stalemate. Now it was being fought in the trenches and the machine gun was king.

But there was also a war in the air — the first airplanes had been used in battle on a large scale. New ideas on bombing from the air — even fighting one another in the air — began to take hold. Pilots on both sides, flying frail, unreliable planes, brought war up into the skies as it had never been fought before.

Another new machine used in the war was Roentgen's X-ray machine. He was hearing reports now that the X rays were being used in hospitals on both sides of the enemy lines. If nothing else, he had helped the soldiers to be treated with X rays in order to find where the steel from the bullets and the mines had charged into their bodies.

In France, he heard, Marie Curie, the widow of Pierre Curie, was driving around to the hospitals with an X-ray machine in the back of an ambulance and helping with the English and French wounded.

It was the only comfort he had now: that in this terrible war his discovery had helped to ease the pain of the wounded and many lives had been saved.

An American, one of Germany's enemies, reported:

BERTHA

We were in the trenches near Toul when we heard that the roentgenologists in the German hospitals were celebrating Roentgen's birthday. The American radiologists appreciate the discovery of the professor as much as the Germans, and we therefore decided on that night to have a little celebration. Yes, we drank with French cognac to the health of the old German professor. They shall not say that we are narrow-minded or prejudiced. We recognize the celebrity of this man; we had a nice evening and only wished that old Professor Roentgen could have heard us.

It seemed that in spite of their governments fighting with each other, the scientists still used each other's information and each other's work.

As the war progressed, Roentgen sensed that everything that he had known since he was a child was disappearing. He had watched Germany grow from a collection of independent states into a majestic country; now it was completely cut down. Few people had jobs — there were fifteen million unemployed — and for those lucky enough to have one, as he was, it was almost impossible to feed a household with his salary. One dollar was the equivalent of about four marks. Yet one pound of bread cost 67 marks, or sixteen dollars; one pound of meat three to four hundred marks, or seventy-five to one hundred dollars; one pound of butter about fourteen hundred forty marks, or three hundred and sixty dollars; and an ordinary suit of clothes between one hundred fifty thousand and two hundred thousand marks, or more than thirty-five thousand dollars!

For Roentgen, like every one else, the mark had little value. But there was even less to buy. He insisted that they use only the small rations of food, and no more. The whole country, starving, had gone on a ration system — each citizen allowed only so much meat, butter, or bread a day. He could stand all that, but he could not stand cutting back on his smoking. Those cheap clay student pipes, filled with the strong Dutch tobacco, were the one luxury he found he could not do without. He was grateful that friends remembered him and sent the tobacco.

As if times were not difficult enough for all of them, Bertha now seemed worse than ever.

They had been married forty-seven years now, and he could not remember what it had been like without her. Nor did he want to find out. In more ways than the world would ever know, she had shared his ideas and never once doubted that he could do whatever he set out to do.

It seemed that Bertha, now eighty-one, could not recover from this last attack of her incurable kidney condition. She lay in bed, her bloated legs and belly filled with fluid, getting weaker day after day.

It is difficult for her to talk or to think and we are always grateful when she can sleep most of the day and all night and if, between times, I can talk to her for short periods. We frequently speak about death, which is not difficult for either of us. I try, of course to avoid telling her my opinion and try to encourage and reassure her.

Her doctors, though, didn't seem to think that this would be Bertha's last illness. Roentgen talked with them on October 24, and they seemed to think that Bertha was slowly getting better. He began to hope for her again.

Bertha died a week later. It was October 31, 1919.

All his fame, all his scientific skill, meant nothing to him now. For the first time in almost fifty years he was lonely.

22

The Lonely Years

What can you say about an eighty-one-year-old woman who just died? That she lived a long and good life? That she loved music and flowers? That she was his best friend and wife for forty-seven years? That, and this was most important of all — that she loved him?

Over the past months he found he had to think about the possibility that Bertha might die. He had even managed to convince himself that he knew how life would be without her. But that was all while Bertha was still alive. Then, no matter how sick she was, Bertha was there, always with him.

Now that it had actually happened, it was all different from what he had imagined it would be. For the first time in almost half a century he was alone, absolutely all alone. And there was nothing he could do about the soundlessness of his house or the silence of his life.

In spite of all his scientific training, his years of working only with facts, he found a way to keep Bertha "alive"

— but only for him. If he tried, if he concentrated enough, he could "see" Bertha just as always, in his mind. What if it did mean blotting out reality, blotting out the facts that had been so important all his life? He didn't care. He liked it better that way. Now, instead of talking directly to Bertha, he would talk to her photographs, or sometimes, read the letters she had written to him years earlier.

He continued to celebrate her birthday, April 22, just as always. For Bertha's birthday, they always ate the first asparagus of the spring season. Sometimes, if they were lucky enough, he found violets to bring to her, the very last of the season. So, on the April after her death, he ate the asparagus and put violets in front of Bertha's photograph — and somehow she knew he was doing it.

He still worked, but now only because he knew it would have pleased Bertha. Besides, there was little else left for him to do. He continued experimenting and writing, but had no heart for either. For example, he found editing some of his writing — always difficult for him — now almost impossible to do.

In one of his letters to Mrs. Theodor Boveri in 1920, he commented

The photograph [of Bertha] helps me at the present time to overcome the reluctance with which I finish the editing of my manuscript; it reminds me of my duty and of my promise and helps me to overcome my inertia. I am sorry that the last of my publications has not turned out to be better and more interesting. If I could rewrite and condense the paper

. . . but I can no longer do it, and on the other hand I can't bring myself to keep these matters to myself.

The day he became seventy-five, March 27, 1920, he received many congratulations from all over the world. There were so many, he believed, because it was also the twenty-fifth anniversary of his discovery of the X ray. Lennep, where he was born, honored him by placing a tablet on his birthplace. The city council of Weilheim named a street in his honor, and later Lennep also named a street after him. But these were all from Prussia, none were from Holland. Somehow, the people from Holland, where he lived as a boy, grew up, and went to school, did not really think of him as one of their own.

A little later that same spring, in 1920, he retired from the university. They gave him permission to use a laboratory in the Physical Institute for as long as he cared to, however. He stayed at Weilheim most of the time now.

Each year, there were fewer and fewer old friends to hear from. Writing to one of these friends, Wölfflin, in March of 1921, he said: "It is especially beneficial for the lonely old man who has lost his life companion and who must live in these sad times, to know that there are still people who remember him in the most intimate way."

Perhaps it was now, as each day passed, that he began to worry more and more: "What will happen to my work after I, too, die?" Perhaps it bothered him that soon, there might be no one he knew left alive to take care of his personal papers. Whom could he trust with all his records, his notes, his letters, and the treasured papers of all his experiments? Perhaps it was then that he put some instructions into his will. They were strange instructions from a man of his fame and scientific brilliance, whose papers should have been saved for history and for others to learn and study from.

Although his long whiskers were white now and he was retired, he tried to keep himself as active as possible. During the summers of 1921 and 1922 he visited Switzerland and took long hikes through the mountains, just as he had done a half-century earlier, when he was a student at the Zurich Polytechnic Institute. Somehow, the power of nature always gave him the strength to carry on; it was almost as if he had to climb those hills and rocks to become recharged again. "This is what I wanted to see once more in my life. This roaring stream is for me the symbol of potential power."

He wrote to his friend, Wölfflin, again:

I would like very much to finish an experimental investigation which I started many months ago, but the walk to the laboratory has gradually become too burdensome for me; I am then too tired when I begin work. Also my vision is not keen enough for the work required. But I am going to make a fresh start.

The Munich press was the first to announce it: "Today at half-past eight A.M., February 10, 1923, His Excellency, Geheimrat Professor Doctor Wilhelm Conrad Roentgen died in his seventy-fifth year after a short illness at Munich. His relatives and friends mourn him deeply.

Cremation will take place on Tuesday, February 13, 1923, at ten o'clock in the morning at the East Cemetery."

Afterwards, his will was read, with its strange request. That request was that all but a few of his scientific papers and personal writings and letters be burned. "Why?" Many wondered. No one really knew. Could it have been tied to his early years, when he had all those troubles in high school, and then in Würzburg as a young teacher? From those early years on, he had trusted only a very few people. Certainly, he never did forget those troubled years.

In his will he gave three hundred and thirty-nine billion paper marks to the poor of the city of Weilheim. It may have sounded like a lot of money, but in those days the mark did not buy very much. He also gave a small amount to their vacation spot of Pontresina. His personal property was carefully distributed among friends by Mrs. Boveri.

But then, came another request, almost as interesting as his order to destroy all his valuable papers. This was to give to the city of Lennep some bonds with "a value of three thousand six hundred and fifty-four gold marks to establish the Professor Doctor Roentgen Foundation." This fund was set up to help only one group of poor and needy in the city of Lennep. They were people he never saw and didn't know, but who might not otherwise be able to finish school and get an education — the teen-age students of the Lennep high school.

132

23

Epilogue:
And Afterwards

Who could resist "seeing" into the invisible? Pictures showing only the skeletons of hands, feet and ribs were spread over newspapers, magazines and even in cartoons.

Most people believed most of what they saw and read, and all of what they heard about those powerful invisible rays. Rumors and facts were all reported alike as truth.

Even stories about the magic powers of X rays were accepted as true scientific fact. In the late nineteenth century, there were many who still believed in magic. They believed X rays were finally their answer to the unseen and unexplainable. These people were still clinging to a centuries-old dream about a magic "something" that would change a worthless stone into a chunk of valuable gold.

Some newspapers helped that belief along by reporting "true" stories of these magic changes. One in Cedar Rapids, Iowa, reported:

George Johnson, a young farmer residing in Jefferson County, a graduate of Columbia College, who has been working with X rays, thinks that he has made a discovery that will startle the world. By means of what he calls X rays, he is enabled to change, in three hours time, a cheap piece of metal worth about thirteen cents to a hundred-fifty-three dollars-worth of gold. The metal so transformed has been tested and pronounced pure gold.

Yet, right along with those half-truths about X rays' magic power were reports from workers who realized that the rays could not perform tricks of magic but could do the unbelievable. Most X rays were able to travel through wood, people, and all but a few metals. Suddenly, what had always been invisible, even with the finest instruments, now became something that could be "looked" into with X rays.

Because of their strange power, X rays swiftly became important in medicine and later in manufacturing and in scientific research.

The new field of medicine that soon appeared was called roentgenology; it used X rays both for diagnosis and for treatment of patients. The doctor working with X rays is called a roentgenologist.

Within just a few weeks of Roentgen's announcement in 1896, a history-making fracture was set by two brothers. On February 3, 1896, at Dartmouth College in Hanover, New Hampshire, the brothers, Dr. Gilman Frost and Dr. Edwin Frost, found the break by X-raying the patient's arm and then were able to set it.

For the first time in man's history, doctors no longer had to guess about what they could not see. Before X rays doctors could only guess where or how a bone was broken. Often the patient was crippled for the rest of his life. But now with X rays, broken bones could be seen as if the doctor were working with a skeleton.

This was the beginning of using X rays to "see" inside the body to help the doctor. The roentgenologists discovered they could use X rays to find something inside the body that should not be there, for instance a swallowed safety pin or nail. And X rays helped them study the parts of the body and how they work, such as the beating of the heart or how food is digested after it is swallowed.

Next they began to use X rays to examine lungs to see if there was any trace of the dreaded lung infection, tuberculosis. They also used X rays to search out any unwanted or unknown growths in the body, called tumors or cancers.

Although the doctors were among the first to see the usefulness of X rays, others quickly joined them. The world quickly and gladly began to use and experiment with X rays, and even to play with them. Writers, poets, salesmen and even entertainers all found a way to use X rays or the information about them in their work. Before long, dentists quickly learned that the rays could be of help to them, too. For the first time, they could "see" into a patient's tooth or jawbone to find and fill a cavity or infection, or if needed, they could X-ray the roots and pull out a tooth.

As it often happens with something new, the first workers using X rays saw no reason to protect themselves against the rays. There was no one to say who should use X rays, how they should be used, what they should be used for, or, even what they really were. But the world began to learn the hard way — through experience.

Thomas Alva Edison, the inventor living in West Orange, New Jersey, was among the first to notice a change in himself. After working with Roentgen rays he complained about a severe pain in his eyes. However, he didn't think that the pain was caused by the direct action of the rays.

Those early X-ray machines were hot, noisy and slow. The pioneers couldn't see or feel the rays, and they believed them to be as harmless as regular light. A chest X ray might take as long as ten minutes, one of the hip perhaps twenty minutes. Also, many a doctor, newly acquainted with the rays, might test his machine to find if it had warmed up by taking a test picture of his own hand.

Some began to notice significant changes in themselves, especially those who kept the rays traveling for a long time. These pioneers reported that their skin was inflamed or burned, or that the rays caused their hair to fall out where the body was exposed to them. And so, the same magazines who earlier announced news of the discovery of the rays now began to tell their readers about the newly discovered dangers. The British *Journal of Photography* on November 13, 1896, carried this story:

William Levy, who was given a Roentgen examination by Professor Jones of the Physical Laboratory of the State University of Minnesota, had the following experience. A picture of his skull was made with a high tension of one hundred thousand volts. On the next day, Mr. Levy began to notice a peculiar effect on the skin wherever it had been most exposed to the rays, and the hair on the right side of his head began to fall out. In a few days this right side of his head was perfectly bald. His right ear had swollen to twice its natural size and presented the same appearance as if it were very badly frozen. Sores were visible on his head, his mouth and throat were blistered so that he could not eat solid food for three weeks and his lips were swollen, cracked and bleeding. Mr. Levy has recovered from the effects of the rays, but still has one-half a bald head.

Another pioneer who was among the first to be damaged was a student at Columbia University. He had been hired to give roentgenologic demonstrations in a New York City department store, Bloomingdale Brothers. In an article in the *Electrical Engineer*, on July 22, 1896, the student, H. D. Hawks, told how he made photographs of the hands of customers with twenty to thirty seconds' exposure, and a picture of the hip in about ten to fifteen minutes. His demonstrations lasted for two or three hours each day, and of course the apparatus was kept running.

At first Hawks noticed an increasing dryness of his skin, which soon began to look like a bad sunburn. Then he noticed the nails on his hands stopped growing and his hair also disappeared at the temples, where he had placed his head close to the tube to show the penetration of the rays through the skull. His eyes were affected and his vision was damaged. The hair of his eyebrows and eyelashes came out. Although he tried to protect himself by using Vaseline and wearing gloves on his hands, nothing seemed to help. . . .

There are many more reports of those earliest pioneers who gave themselves bad burns because they did not know enough about X rays. All began to notice that the rays produced an inflammation of the skin, or caused the hair to fall out. Most could not even begin to guess at what other damage the rays could be doing to them.

Years later, in 1936, a plain stone monument would be placed at the Roentgen Institute in Hamburg, Germany. It would carry a dedication: "To the roentgenologists of all nations who have given their lives in the struggle against diseases of mankind." There would be one hundred and ten names carved on the stone, and more would be added through the years.

What could be done with all this unexpected damage? One researcher had an idea. The damaging effect of X rays could be turned around to help people. He reasoned that the Roentgen rays could be used to get rid of something unwanted on the body. And so, Dr. L. Fruend was one of the first to find the second important use of X rays in medicine: the rays could be used to destroy unwanted growths on the body. Instead of harming people, the rays would help them.

One of Dr. Fruend's first subjects was a little girl who was so badly disfigured by a tremendous furlike birthmark that her parents insisted that the hair be removed. Dr. Fruend gave her X-ray treatments each day for two hours for a period of ten days. On the tenth day, the hair came out. There, on the girl's neck was a small circular bald spot.

Of course, today we know that Dr. Fruend's dose was far, far too great. But from this beginning grew the idea of using X rays in medicine to treat certain special skin diseases and cancer.

But the doctors knew they had many problems if they were to use X rays to help treat the sick. What was the right amount of X rays to use? How long should a patient be exposed to them? Too much would burn the skin, but too little would not work at all. Also, how could they best protect the healthy part of the body while using X rays?

Much of what they would learn over the years came only from experience itself. As time went on, many of the workers began to realize that they as well as their patients were in danger from X rays. Soon workers began to take special care when working with the rays. Before long, X-ray equipment was housed in special rooms lined with lead to keep the rays from traveling through them. Also, the workers around the machine were protected by special clothes and by lead or lead-glass shields.

It was only an accident that Roentgen himself was protected. In order to get better experiments he had used a big zinc-lined box, and later a lead plate, when working with the rays.

And while the doctors were busily learning what they could about using X rays, others, just a little later, began to find them useful, too. Researchers and people in business also used X rays as a tool to tell about what something is made of, and why it behaves in its own special way.

In business, particularly in manufacturing, X rays were used to find trouble spots invisible to the eye or to avoid problems before they could get started.

Before manufacturers began using X rays, they had a different way of finding out how good their items were. In those earlier days, certain items could only be spot checked. That meant about a dozen would be taken from a large batch and examined. But there was no way to be sure that the other pieces in that same batch were all right. It just had to be taken for granted that the others were free from defects.

The system of spot-checking worked fairly well in the beginning, but as the years wore on, and there were more and more products coming off factory assembly lines, a more definite way of safety checking had to be found. Today, people expect that their complicated television set, or electric toaster, or car, or, even, long-range missile with over three hundred thousand parts, will work perfectly. The manufacturers, too, found that it is cheaper in the long run to build a good product than a poor one.

But testing an item to be sure it was free from defects often meant that it would have to be taken apart — piece by piece — or cut open. Of course, just by doing that, it would be destroyed. So, over the years, manufacturers have found different ways to test something without destroying it. This is called, "nondestructive testing." X rays are one way to test something by "nondestructive testing."

A radiograph is an image or a picture produced by the action of an X ray on a photographic plate. By taking radiographs, manufacturers can check something for weak spots or defects without ever taking it apart.

The testers know that some of the X rays are able to travel through objects, while other rays are soaked up. The amount going through depends upon the energy of the rays, what kind of thing they are traveling through, and its thickness. For example, steel is checked for an invisible air bubble, called a void, which is below the surface. Because more rays will be able to travel through the void, that area will appear darker on the film when it is developed. By looking at the dark spots, the inspectors will know that there are defects in the piece of steel; something they could not "see" any other way.

Nondestructive testing has been a part of business for more than thirty years. The airlines of the United States probably use more nondestructive testing in the maintenance of their equipment than any other form of transportation. X rays are an important part of their safety checks. For this one industry alone, X rays are used on the structure of the plane where it is impractical to do the inspection any other way. The rays are used to search out any faults on wing and center section spars, skin and fittings,

141

also fuel line, fuel nozzles, in engine cases with two or three layers, and many other parts of the plane.

For instance, one airline reported trouble with electric wires breaking off inside a molded rubber plug used on food warmers while the plane was aloft. They had some instances where the rubber plug actually caught on fire. No airline wants the smoke and smell of burning rubber filling the cabin and worrying the passengers. By means of X rays they were able not only to pick out plugs that had one strand of wire broken, but were able to detect the design and manufacturing errors that caused the plugs to burn.

Many industries today use X rays to find flaws or damage that could go undiscovered. The rays are used to examine plastics, rubber insulation, ship hulls, railroad tracks, tanks under pressure, automobiles, gun barrels, ball bearings, radio tubes, coal, rubber tires, golf balls, wood, even porcelain eggs, and of course, all the thousands of parts that make up the rockets and rocket motors sent up by the United States to the moon. Today, X rays are used to examine packed suitcases or other items carried on airplanes or sent through the mail to be sure they contain nothing illegal.

In research, X rays are used by scientists in a different way from either the doctors or the business people. They are used in research dealing with astronomy, laser science and space navigation. New equipment using X rays has been developed. Today we have microscopes, counter-gauges, stereoscopic moving pictures, all of which use X rays. A whole new field of measurement began because of X-ray diffraction, the bending of the rays by certain crystals.

Of course, there are a great many different kinds of X-ray equipment. The machines may vary in size from the small portable ones easily carried by one man to huge ones which take pictures of part of a plane or part of a spaceship.

And yet, with all that X rays meant to the world, from the beginning, Wilhelm Conrad Roentgen wanted no part of them. He considered X rays as only one of his many experiments. He was content to step aside and let others use his discovery. He never earned any money directly from the later uses of X rays nor did he want any part of the money made by others. In the tradition of the true scientist, he believed his discovery of X rays should belong to the world.

Even his will showed his strong feelings about the world. Why should this successful scientist give money in his will to poor and needy high school students wanting an education? Students that he never met. Was it that he never forgot how difficult a world run by adults' rules and regulations could be? Only someone who knew how Wilhelm Conrad Roentgen himself struggled to get an education could try to guess why.

His own difficult high school years might also help explain that other strange request he made in his will — that all his and Bertha's notes and letters be burned. The flaming pile included all their personal papers, business letters, even his scientific notes. All their written thoughts, opinions, theories, guesses, points of view, ideas, dreams and even feelings were destroyed by fire.

Today, the only remains of either Wilhelm or Bertha Roentgen's papers are copies of his published scientific reports and the letters they sent to friends who were wise enough to keep them.

Perhaps with this last request, Wilhelm Conrad Roentgen tried to separate his wife and himself from a world he never quite trusted. Yet, though he wanted to separate himself from the world, he would always be part of it.

He was one of the few scientists to become well known to people outside science. His discovery of X rays began a scientific revolution; it started a rush of ideas, new inventions, and created changes in medicine and in science.

When Wilhelm Conrad Roentgen selected the letter "X" — which in science stands for the unknown — to name his rays, he may not have known what they were or what to do with them. But the world seized his discovery, quickly caught onto the way to see into the invisible, and has been finding out about itself ever since.